THE COMPLETE GUIDE TO CHOOSING A
PERFORMANCE
BICYCLE

THE COMPLETE GUIDE TO CHOOSING A
PERFORMANCE BICYCLE

John Lehrer

Introduction by Ray Keener

Principal Photographer, Steve Broaddus

A Running Press/Friedman Group Book
Running Press Book Publishers
Philadelphia, Pennsylvania

A RUNNING PRESS/FRIEDMAN GROUP BOOK

9 8 7 6 5 4 3 2 1

Digit on the right indicates the number of this printing.

Library of Congress Cataloguing-in-Publication Data
Lehrer, John.
    The complete guide to choosing a performance bicycle.
    "A Running Press/Friedman Group Book."
    Bibliography: p.
    Includes index.
    1. Bicycles—Purchasing. I. Title.
TL410.L39 1988   629.2'272'029   87-43103
ISBN 0-89471-588-7
ISBN 0-89471-587-9 (pbk.)

THE COMPLETE GUIDE TO CHOOSING A PERFORMANCE BICYCLE
was prepared and produced by
Michael Friedman Publishing Group, Inc
15 West 26th Street
New York, New York 10010

Editor: Nancy Kalish
Editorial Assistant: Sharon Kalman
Copy Editor: Meredith Greene
Art Director: Mary Moriarty
Designer: Robert W. Kosturko
Photo Editors: Philip Hawthorne and Christine Cancelli
Production Manager: Karen L. Greenberg

Typeset by Lettering Directions, Inc.
Color separations by South Seas Graphic Arts Company
Printed and bound in Hong Kong by Leefung-Asco Printers Ltd.

This book may be ordered from the Publisher.
Please include $1.50 postage.
But try your bookstore first.

Running Press Book Publishers
125 South Twenty-second Street
Philadelphia, Pennsylvania 19103

ACKNOWLEDGMENTS

I'm especially grateful to Cheri Wolpert, whose love and support have made a tremendous difference both to my writing and my life; also to my good friend Ray Keener, who made major contributions to the sections of the book on bike sales and bike fit, and who reviewed the entire manuscript with me. Without Cheri and Ray, I would not have been able to write this book. I'd also like to gratefully acknowledge the technical assistance of the staff at Two Wheel Transit of Huntington Beach, California, and the staff of Marina Del Rey Bike Shop in Marina Del Rey, California, who provided the equipment and the setting for many of the photographs.

Thanks and love also go to my parents, John W. Lehrer and Janis Lehrer, for their continuing support, and to my good friends and cycling pals Pete Chaffey, Bob Howells, Alice Mendoza, Casey Patterson, and Jeff Spencer.

John A. Lehrer
Topanga, California
June 1987

CONTENTS

John Lehrer

So you're going to buy a bicycle. If you haven't shopped for a new bike in several years, be prepared for a barrage of new terms and technologies. The lugged steel frame, the accepted standard since the turn of the century, is no longer your only choice. Componentry has evolved as well. Bikes now have handlebar-mounted computers, quick-release pedals, treadless tires, and indexed shifting.

Does sorting out all of these new technologies sound intimidating? Are you the type of consumer who dreads buying equipment you don't really understand? Are you afraid that you'll spend more than $500 on a bicycle and end up with the "wrong thing"?

Not to worry. Despite the recent high-tech developments in bicycle frame construction and componentry, purchasing a new bicycle continues to be a very *human* process. In my 12 years of owning and managing bike shops, I've discovered that the best approach to buying a bike is to forget about becoming an "expert" and simply trust your judgment. Find a bike shop with people you can relate to and let the nuts and bolts of buying a bike take care of themselves.

The importance of person-to-person contact involved in bicycle buying results from one simple fact: Bicycle shops, unlike the bicycles they sell, are not much different from those in the days of Orville and Wilbur Wright, America's best-known former bike peddlers.

Bicycle retailing is a veritable backwater of American capitalism.

Although the leading shops in major markets are as sophisticated as any specialty retailer, the dehumanizing aspects of buying consumer goods have not yet invaded the bicycle shop. People own and work in bike shops because they love bicycles, not because they expect to make a lot of money.

Consider these questions: When was the last time you saw a television commercial seductively and subliminally pushing bicycles? Have you ever been in a shop that's part of a nationwide chain, with no sign of the store's owner? Franchising, with its uniform stores full of prepackaged goods, and faceless, interchangeable employees, has invaded nearly all retail markets. In bike shops, though, the "employee uniform" is still greasy hands and shaved legs.

When it comes to buying a bicycle, *where* you buy is at least as important as *what* you buy. This is a mind-boggling concept to the American consumer. When you purchase a hamburger or a soft drink, you think of the brand you want—where you buy it becomes a formality. It's ironic that when shopping for a bicycle, which costs 500 times more than a burger or a cola, the person and the store selling you the product are at least as important—and sometimes more so—as the product itself.

In a recent survey of sophisticated bicycle consumers, cyclists were asked to identify the qualities that led them to prefer one bicycle store over another. Nearly two-thirds of the respondents rated "knowledgeable staff" as *extremely important*, while such factors that would be expected to rate highly in other retail businesses, such as large inventory, brand names carried, and convenient location, were mentioned by less than one-third of those surveyed. Would consumers expect or desire a knowledgeable staff at their McDonald's, K-Mart, or Safeway?

The typical first-time quality bike purchaser wants to thoroughly understand the product before he or she makes a decision. This desire for greater understanding leads to a tour of local bike shops, hours spent digesting and rehashing component specifications, and ultimately, massive confusion. I can spot this type of customer the minute they walk in the front door—the blank gaze, the shuffling gait, the slack jaw. The first words out of their mouth are always, "I'm confused. Last week you told me...and then the guy at the other shop said...but then I read in the magazine that..."

The prospective bike consumer has been barraged with so many different *opinions* that he's unable to make a decision. The key to an anxiety-free bicycle purchase is to dodge opinions as if they were bullets. What you want and need from a bicycle is *enjoyment*. "The correct" frame and component specifications won't make you happy. Assuming that the bike you're about to purchase is the right size and is suited to your riding style, the *color* may well be more important to you than the brand name! Once you are convinced to spend more than $300 for a bicycle, it's hard to go wrong. Try not to learn too much about bikes, and you'll stay out of trouble.

Here's my formula for anxiety-free bike buying: Read John Lehrer's *The Complete Guide to Choosing a Performance Bicycle*. Talk to cyclists who do the same type of riding you'd like to do. Ask them about their favorite shops, and why they like them. Narrow the list down to two stores. Visit these stores at least twice, and talk to different people each time. Find a shop employee you like and trust. Buy the bike they recommend to suit your needs and budget, and the one that feels good when you test-ride it. Make sure you like the color.

The book you are about to read is almost completely free of opinions. Rather, John Lehrer's approach is systematic and factual with an emphasis on buying the right bicycle for your *human* needs—not just your riding needs —plus a few tips on how to get the most out of it. Don't get bogged down in component specifications and other overly technical trappings of cycling. Read this book instead to form your opinions and learn how to trust your experience—you'll end up with the right bike and more time to enjoy it!

> —Ray Keener,
> Boulder, Colorado, 1987

Analyzing Your Riding Needs

When you decide to buy a quality bicycle and become a cyclist, you're entering an exciting and varied world, full of interesting people, activities, and equipment. If some of this world seems complicated and a bit intimidating, don't worry—it needn't be. You can get involved as little or as much as you want and still enjoy cycling, and you can do it at your own pace and in your own style.

Cycling combines thinking and feeling, the intellectual and the sensual. And that's never more true than when you take the first step— buying a new bicycle. Walk into a bike shop and you're likely to be overwhelmed by the various styles and colors of the bicycles lined up on the floor or stacked along the walls, to say nothing of cycling equipment. You'll be bombarded with an endless assortment of jerseys, shorts, shoes, helmets, gloves, and tools. How can you make sense of it all and get what you want from cycling? What's the best way to avoid making unnecessary mistakes?

To get the right start in bicycling, you have to have a clear understanding of who you are and what you expect from the sport. But before we get into that, let's clear up some misconceptions you may have about bicycles.

One of the best things about cycling is that virtually *anyone*—young or old, male or female—can enjoy and benefit from it. But first you have to understand who you are and what you want from the sport.

David B. Keith

Jeffrey E. Blackman

First, while it's true that bicycles and cycling gear are more complicated than the equipment used in some sports—running, for example—bicycles are still relatively simple devices. Almost everything about a bicycle is exposed, accessible, and right on the surface where you can see it. If you want to take the time, you can easily figure out how every part of a bicycle works.

Second, you can enjoy cycling and be sure that you get a well-made, responsive, reliable bicycle without having to buy the most expensive bike in your local shop. As long as you're willing to spend at least $300, you can be sure you'll get a good bike regardless of the brand. The bicycle business is very competitive, and you

pretty much get what you pay for. But you do need to know why some bicycles cost more than others. One of the major purposes of this book is to help you understand exactly what you get for your money and how to decide what meets your needs and desires.

Third, no single bicycle suits every person or every purpose. You have to be realistic about your needs, the kind of person you are and the kind of riding you think you want to do. The best bike is the one that fits you personally—your body, your budget, your riding needs, even your sense of color and style. Remember, buying a bike is an emotional as well as rational decision. Follow your head *and* your heart. If you're systematic about the rational aspects of buying

your bicycle, you'll be more likely to get a bike you love to ride.

Buying the right bike begins with *you*. Don't even walk into a bike shop until you've thought a good deal about the kind of person you are. That will determine the right kind of bike for you as much as your cycling experience thus far. If you walk into a shop and tell a salesperson that you're interested in buying a bike but need help in deciding which one, the salesperson might ask you how much and what kind of riding you're planning to do. Those may seem like sensible questions, but for many people they aren't very useful, because someone new to adult cycling or just getting back into it after a decade's layoff might not have any idea how much or

Jeffrey E. Blackman

David Madison

Do you like to tinker with the equipment you buy? Are you competitive? Do you have to have "the best" when you go shopping? The answers to these kinds of questions will help you find the bike that's right for you.

what kind of riding he or she is going to do.

There are other, more helpful questions that you can ask yourself before you visit a shop:

Are you a mechanically oriented person? Will you want to tinker with your bike, take parts off it, scrub them with a toothbrush and put the whole thing back together? Or are you going to want your bike shop to perform all the servicing on your bike? Does the idea of buying new and better components and putting them on your bike appeal to you?

If you're someone who's always taking things apart, you might want to buy a bike that has a good frame but whose components (some or all of them) aren't equal to the frame's

quality. That's because you're the kind of person who will want to upgrade the components at some point anyway, customizing the bike to suit your interests or needs at the time. On the other hand, if you think you'll rely on a shop to do your maintenance, you probably will want to buy a bike whose frame and components are of similar quality.

Are you a competitive person? If so, you may be happiest with a racing bike. But you may say, I don't have any interest in racing. That's not the point; very few cyclists do. The question is, if you see someone up ahead of you on a bike, do you have a strong urge to catch (and pass) him or her?

Similarly, what's your athletic background? Are you a fitness-oriented

person? Maybe you're thinking of entering a triathlon or using your new bike to ride centuries (100-mile rides) or time trials (a race against the clock). Maybe you want to join a competitive cycling club. All of these considerations will have a bearing on the type of bike you'll most enjoy.

On the surface, some of the questions you should ask yourself before deciding on a bike might seem to have nothing to do with bicycles:

How often do you buy a car? Do you buy a new one every couple of years—a different one, a better one—or do you buy a Volvo, run it into the ground, and then buy another one? The first type of person may want to buy a $300 bike initially, because he or she will ride it for a

Joe McNally/Wheeler Pictures

couple of years, then buy a $500 bike, ride it for awhile, then buy an $800 bike. This approach to buying a bike lets people discover gradually what they need and prefer in a bike. By the time they get to the third bike, they'll know from their riding experience exactly the kind of frame and components they want. This is preferable to taking well-intentioned, but sometimes inappropriate, advice from a bike shop.

Conversely, someone who doesn't like to "trade up" in cars, houses, or sporting equipment will want to be even more careful in choosing the right bike the first time.

Some questions you should ask yourself refer directly to bicycles:

What was your last bicycle like? If you haven't ridden a bicycle for a decade or more, you might find the handling of a racing bicycle a little unstable and scary, preferring instead the comfort and stability of a touring or mountain bike. On the other hand, if you've been riding an inexpensive 10-speed for the past few years, the switch to a more responsive bike might be just what you're looking for.

How often do you think you'll ride? Also, what's your idea of a long bike ride? If you think that you'll only ride ten to twenty miles once a week, there's probably no point in buying a $1200 bike; it will last longer than you will. If, however, you plan to use a bicycle as a way to maintain fitness, you may want to spend more than the minimum amount necessary to get a decent bike. There's no point in buying a flimsy excuse not to exercise!

Do you take care of your equipment? Do you abuse it or quickly wear it out? This is a very important question, because as bicycles become more expensive they also become more durable in some ways and more fragile in others. It might be foolish to spend $800 on a bicycle if you're not going to take care of it; on the other hand, if you use your sporting equipment hard but also take the time to maintain it, it makes sense to spend more money on a bicycle in order to get more durable, better-quality bearings and components.

There are, of course, two questions to ask yourself that have nothing intrinsically to do with cycling but are of crucial importance:

Are you on a strict budget? You may be surprised at the price of even a good entry-level adult bike; it may cost three times what you paid for the bike you rode as a child or what a similar bicycle would have cost ten years ago. (Not in real dollars, though; bicycles are better values than ever.) Still, some people are shocked to find a good entry-level bike priced at $300–$400. You'll probably also need to allot another $100–$200 for cycling equipment and accessories. (Keep in mind that any discussion of price is in terms of the dollar's value in mid-1987.)

Finally, the question that can smash all your previous considerations to smithereens, making all ruminations thus far irrelevant:

Bikes come in all shapes, sizes, and colors, and they're designed for a wide variety of purposes—touring, commuting, recreational riding, training for fitness and competition, to name just a few.

Jeffrey E. Blackman

Jeffrey E. Blackman

Do you want the best of everything? When you get involved in a sport or hobby, do you enjoy fine equipment for its own sake? Will you always pick the BMW over the Toyota? This question has more to do with *wants* and *desires* than needs, and it's a valid consideration.

You'll really have to search your soul on this one. Some people can ride 200 miles a week on a $300 bike and be perfectly happy; others only want to ride twenty miles a week but have to have an $800 bike. And plenty of people who can't afford to spend $40,000 on a sports car will buy (and thoroughly enjoy) a $1200 bicycle instead. As a true cycling aficionado once put it, "I've never bought a bike that was too expensive—that I didn't think was worth it." If, when you wander down the rows of bicycles in your favorite shop, you immediately notice and appreciate the fine quality of the finish on the components of bikes priced $800 and up, it's a good indication that you like to own the best. Beware of falling under the spell of SBL (severe bike lust)!

The point is, if you have stronger desires than you have needs, you have even more reason to get good advice when buying a bike. Starting off with a $1200 bike precludes learning from your own long-term experience.

These are the kinds of questions you have to ask yourself, for at least one reason: The people who work in bike shops are generally concerned about helping you as well as being enthusiastic and knowledgeable about bicycles. But they aren't always professionally trained salespeople. So it's up to you to do your homework ahead of time. Otherwise, there's a good chance that you won't get good advice, which may lead to your buying a bike that's not right for you.

If you know exactly why you want to buy a bike, you can go to the bike shop with the right questions; then, if the salesperson isn't doing a particularly good job or tries to sell you something you don't want, you're in a position to guide him or her rather than being led around by the nose and wasting your time.

On the other hand, if you don't do

Sport bikes are versatile machines that can be used for light touring, recreational riding, and beginning competition. The Univega Gran Rally (about $625) is a good example of a mid-priced production sport bike.

Univega

Steve Broaddus

enough thinking ahead of time, you're dependent on the abilities (or lack thereof) of the salesperson. You may end up walking out of the shop because the bike that the salesperson has shown you isn't what you want, and you're not sure why. Or, you buy what he or she tells you to buy and later find out it isn't what you wanted at all. The lesson is, don't let the salesperson do your whole job for you.

Okay, you've looked at yourself and have an idea of your cycling wants and needs. Next, what are your choices? What kind of bikes are available?

There are three major categories of bicycle—sport, racing, and mountain bikes—and three minor categories—touring, triathlon, and city bikes—to choose from.

Sport bikes—Also called sport/touring or recreational bikes, sport bikes make up the largest category of "serious" adult bicycles; sport bikes range in price from about $300 to more than $1000, although most fall between $300 and $800. Sport bikes comprise the "happy medium" between touring and racing bikes—

they're moderately responsive, comfortable, and reasonably lightweight. Their gearing is low enough for beginning and intermediate riders. They're the best choice for most people and most road-riding applications—recreational riding, fitness riding, light touring, commuting, triathlons, centuries, and club rides.

Racing bikes—Racing bikes, sometimes called "pro" bikes, are lighter and more responsive, or quick-handling, than sport bikes; because of their steeper frame angles and narrower tires, they feel stiff and slightly harsh to ride compared to sport bikes. Their gearing is usually appropriate for strong, experienced riders. Racing bikes range in price from $300 to more than $3000; most cost more than $800. Almost all bare framesets you see hanging from the walls of pro bike shops are waiting to be built up into racing bikes.

Mountainbikes — Mountainbikes, also called all-terrain bikes or ATBs, were invented in Marin County, California, in the mid-1970s and were first mass-produced in 1982. Since

Over the past several years, mountain bikes have been the hottest-selling type of bicycle, garnering a bigger share of the market each year. One of the best you can buy is the Mt. Tam (about $1,500) from Fisher MountainBikes.

then, their popularity has grown explosively; in 1987, mountain bike sales made up 40–50 percent of the sales of many quality bike shops. As it turns out, most people ride mountain bikes almost exclusively on the road. Their comfortable, upright riding position and ultra-low gears make them "bikes for all seasons." Mountain bikes range in price from $300 to more than $2000; most cost between $300 and $700.

One of the first big decisions you'll have to make—if you haven't realized it already—is whether to buy a road bike or a mountain bike. If you want to ride anywhere off-road besides smooth dirt or fire roads, of course, the choice is simple. A mountain bike is the only way to go—it has the right tires, frame design, and gearing to handle any terrain in style.

For riding the roads, the decision isn't so simple; both mountain bikes and road bikes are suitable for the job. There are probably three key considerations. First, mountain bikes are easier to control because of their fat tires, relaxed frame geometry, and upright handlebars (which put the controls at your fingertips and pro-

John Lehrer

(Below) In 1982, the Stumpjumper by Specialized became the first mass-produced mountain bike to hit American shores. The 1987 version is a far better bike, and it costs less (about $650). (Right) You wanted to know where they came up with a name like "Stumpjumper"...?

Courtesy of Specialized Bicycle Components

duce an upright sitting position). Second, mountain bikes stand up to abuse better than road bikes, and their tires are virtually impervious to flats on the street. In other words, for many beginning cyclists a mountain bike is less frustrating to own. If these factors are important, you might opt for a mountain bike.

The third principal consideration is riding distance. If you plan to go out for hour-long rides, a mountain bike is fine. For distances longer than about fifteen miles, however, mountain bikes just aren't as comfortable as road bikes. You can't vary your hand position as much as on a road bike, the upright seating position puts too much weight on your rear end, and the fat tires produce higher rolling resistance.

If you're just getting back into cycling, there are two ways to go when it comes to the mountain bike-road bike choice (assuming that both appeal to you). If you think that you might want to ride centuries in a year or so, for example, you could buy a road bike. Or you could buy a mountain bike now, ride it for a year, and then buy a road bike. Chances are,

you'd still have plenty of use for your mountain bike—for trail riding, commuting, errands, as a second bike for friends to ride, and so on.

Sport, racing, and mountain bikes are the three main types you'll find on the floors of most quality bike shops (also called "enthusiasts'" or "pro" shops). There are three other, more specialized, bikes you might want to consider, too:

Touring bikes—True touring bikes have long wheelbases, triple chain rings, heavy-duty wheels and tires, and cantilever brakes. They're designed for carrying heavy loads (thirty to sixty pounds or more) over hilly and flat terrain, and over good and bad roads. There are less than two dozen touring models available, principally because most people find that they can do short tours (overnights and weekends, even week-long trips) on sport or mountain bikes. You can go fast and have fun on a touring bike; don't discount them just because they're not flashy.

Triathlon bikes—It's hard to know whether there is such a thing as a true "triathlon" bike. Sure, there are "funny bikes" with longhorn han-

Real touring bikes, like the Nishiki Cresta GT (about $550) are pretty rare these days. You can spot the genuine article by its triple crankset, cantilever brakes, and braze-ons for racks and extra water bottles.

Steve Broaddus

The Scott Tinley triathlon bike is one of three bikes in the Raleigh Technium series, which combines steel and aluminum tubing in a high-tech frame at a reasonable cost.

dlebars, disc rear wheels, small front wheels, and forward-sloping top tubes that world-class triathletes (and would-be world-class triathletes) ride. But most bikes that are billed as triathlon bikes differ very little from sport bikes—basically, they're slightly less rigid and responsive than flat-out racing bikes.

City bikes—City bikes are urban mountain bikes—less expensive but relatively rugged bikes that are intended for life on the road. Superficially, they look like mountain bikes. The frame design is the same, as are the fat tires, handlebars, and cantilever brakes, but the tires don't have a tread pattern designed for good traction in the dirt, and city bikes usually have only two chain rings instead of the triples that are typical of genuine mountain bikes. City bikes are good, less-expensive alternatives to mountain bikes for people who never intend to ride off-road in a serious way.

Now you should be able to determine what kind of bikes are available, and how to decide what best suits your needs and desires. In the next chapter, we'll discuss what you get for your money and how to decide how much to spend for a bicycle.

Courtesy of Schwinn Bicycle Co.

Not everyone who likes the look of a mountain bike needs a genuine off-roader. Since most riders who buy mountain bikes do almost all their riding on the street anyway, many will be perfectly happy with a bike like this Schwinn Mirada (about $290), a city bike that has some of the features found on all-terrain bikes; a triple crankset, bear-trap pedals, cantilever brakes, thumb shifters, and fat tires. This type of bike is suitable for riding on hard-packed dirt roads, too. It will perform well anywhere except when you need knobby tires for traction, such as in loose dirt or for climbing steep hills off-road.

How To Decide Which Bike Is Right For You

There has never been a better time to buy a bike. Quality and selection are better than ever, and technical developments that were found only on top-of-the-line bikes just a few years ago have made their way down to entry-levels models. Today, bicycling is truly technology gone *right*, the perfect combination of man and machine.

In 1987, American consumers could choose from nearly five hundred different models of quality adult bicycles—racing bikes, sport bikes, mountain bikes, touring bikes, and city bikes. What's a prospective owner of a new bike to do in the face of choices like that? Never fear: The purpose of this chapter is to help you sort through this vast array of two-wheeled machinery.

In order to make an intelligent, informed decision, you need to know the answers to a number of questions: How do bicycles differ from one another? What makes a bicycle ride and feel the way it does? If I spend more money on a bicycle, what do I get for it? The answers to these questions can help you narrow the range of bicycles from which you'll ultimately select the one that's just right for you.

First, let's break a bicycle down into its two most important elements: the *frame* and the *components*.

BICYCLE FRAMES

The essential structural configuration of the bicycle frame (often referred to as the "diamond" frame) has changed little in the past century. The materials and technology used to produce frames have changed tremendously, however. The high-quality frames on the bicycles you'll be considering are produced in the Orient (Japan and Taiwan), Europe, and the United States. Some are made by hand, but the majority are manufactured on automated brazing machines. The means of production, however, is less important than the intregrity and precise alignment of the final product.

The two most important things you need to know about a bicycle frame are its *geometry* and its *composition*.

Frame geometry

A bicycle frame's geometry—the configuration of tube lengths, dimensions, and angles—is primarily what determines how it rides and handles. Geometry affects whether a bike feels stable or quick-handling, comfortable or harsh, responsive or sluggish. It affects how a bike feels climbing a hill, and how it corners. The combination of frame geometry and tubing materials, which we'll get to shortly, allows a bike designer to specify frames for any purpose.

You can make yourself crazy trying to understand the details of bicycle frame design; hard-core bike junkies will argue endlessly about how a particular head tube angle or amount of fork rake will affect bike handling. Even experienced frame builders disagree on such issues. If you want to learn the lingo to satisfy your curiosity or impress bike shop employees, fine. But it won't help you enjoy riding your bike a whit more; what's worse, getting wrapped up in an excess of technical talk has the effect of "mystifying" bicycle design and frame building. If you get sucked into this trap from the start, you're liable to feel either that the whole subject is too complicated for you to understand, or that unless you have a bike with specific dimensions (down to

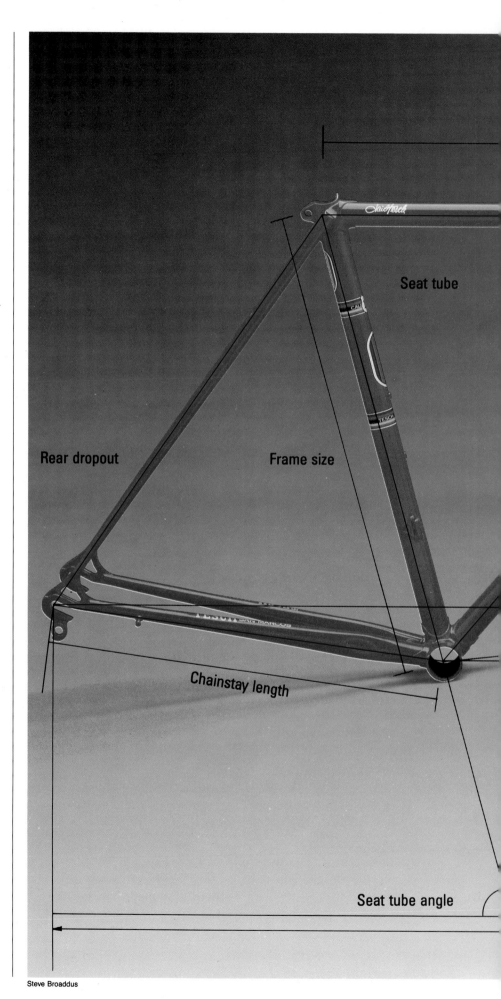

Seat tube

Rear dropout

Frame size

Chainstay length

Seat tube angle

Steve Broaddus

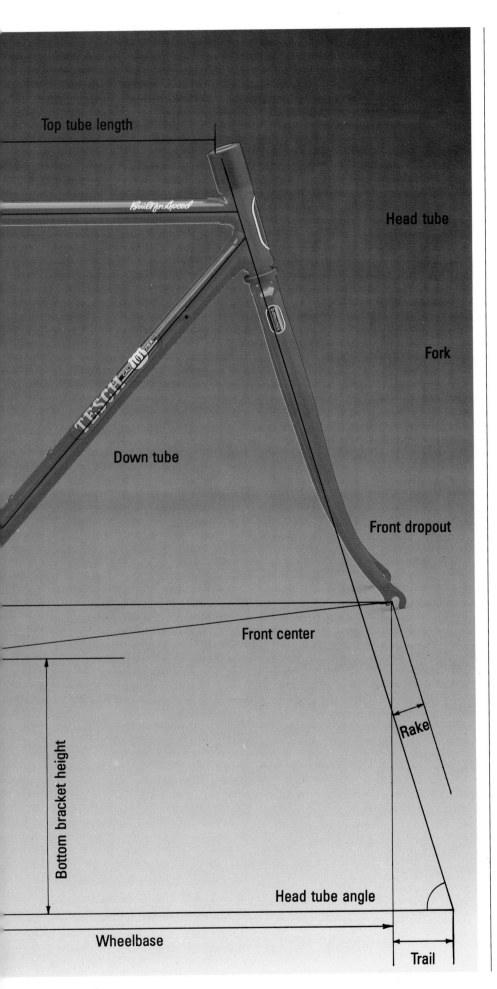

the fraction of a centimeter), your riding will suffer.

Your first concern should not be with geometric esoterica, but with whether a particular bike fits you. That's determined primarily by seat tube length and top tube length; we'll discuss how to buy the right size frame in the next chapter.

Meanwhile, the following information is all most people need to know about frame geometry:

Head tube angle—Head tube angles range from shallow (69 degrees, found on some mountain bikes), to moderate (73 degrees, found on many sport bikes), to steep (75 degrees, found on some racing bikes). A bike's head tube angle works together with fork rake to influence a bike's handling. In general, the steeper the head tube angle, the more responsive and quick-handling a bike will be. A steeper head tube angle also makes a bike somewhat more rigid and less comfortable.

Fork rake—Touring bikes and mountain bikes generally have the most fork rake; racing bikes have the least. More fork rake produces more low-speed stability, which tourists (with heavy loads), mountain bikers (riding over varied, uneven terrain), and novice riders find reassuring. Racers and those riders who appreciate high-speed and responsiveness opt for bikes with less fork rake.

Wheelbase—Racing bikes have short wheelbases, about 39 inches (99 centimeters); touring and mountain bikes have long wheelbases, about 43 inches (109 centimeters); sport bikes fall somewhere in between. Short wheelbases make a bike quick-turning and rigid; long wheelbases contribute to comfort and stability.

Chain stay length—Short chain stays shorten a bike's wheelbase and make the rear triangle more rigid, improving acceleration. Because they shift a rider's weight over the rear wheel more, short chain stays help a bike climb better. Racing bikes have the shortest chain stays, about 16 inches (41 centimeters); the chain stays on sport bikes are about 17 inches (43 centimeters) long; mountain bikes and touring bikes may have chain stays longer than 18 inches (45 centimeters).

25

Other considerations—The seat tube angle, trail, front center, and other dimensions—affect the way a bike responds, too. But there is less agreement about these factors.

The general trend in bicycle design over the past five years has been to make all bicycles (racing, sport, and mountain) lighter, more quick-handling, and responsive.

Frame composition

Quality bicycle frames are made from steel, aluminum, composite (carbon fiber), and titanium tubing. Each has different properties that make it more or less suitable for use on a bicycle.

Steel—The overwhelming majority of quality bicycle frames are made from a high-strength chrome-molybdenum or manganese-molybdenum alloy steel tubing, because it's relatively cheap, easy to bond together (by welding or brazing), strong, rigid, and fatigue-resistant. On the negative side, steel corrodes relatively easily (there's no inexpensive, effective way to prevent it from doing so), and steel is relatively heavy compared to other frame materials of the same strength. The best steel tubing is *butted*, meaning that the walls of the tubing are thicker at the ends, where stresses are greater, and thinner in the middle. Butted tubing is lighter and more resilient than straight-gauge tubing of similar strength. Some of the better-known brands of high-quality steel tubing are Reynolds, Columbus, Tange (pronounced tăn-gāy), Ishiwata, and True Temper. Until a few years ago, all butted tubing was seamless, but recently butted seamed tubing has been used in the construction of bicycle frames. The highest quality seamed tubing (Tange 900, 1000, and Infinity; Ishiwata IXO and EX; Columbus Tenax; and Reynolds 501) is almost identical in strength and function to seamless tubing, but it costs much less. Complete bikes with steel frames range from $300 to $3000.

Aluminum—In the last five years, aluminum in several configurations has become popular as a frame material. For example, you'll find bikes made from oversize, welded aluminum tubing such as those produced by Cannondale and Klein. Also popular are frames made from standard or nearly standard size tubing, such as those made by Alan, Vitus, and Trek; the tubes are glued and/or screwed together. Raleigh makes several bicycles whose main triangles are made from aluminum tubing but whose seat stays, chain stays, and forks are steel. As techniques have become perfected, the price of aluminum frames has come down. You can buy an aluminum bicycle starting at about $400; you can also pay upward of $3000 for some aluminum bikes.

Aluminum-frame bicycles ride differently from steel-frame bicycles; they also ride differently from one another depending on the diameter and wall thickness of the tubing used. Oversized-tube aluminum bicycles tend to be rigid and efficient, giving what some riders consider a slightly harsh ride. Bicycles with frames made of conventional-diameter tubing give a more comfortable, slightly flexy or springy ride. If you weigh less than 120 pounds, you'll probably prefer the ride of an aluminum bike with conventional-diameter tubing; on the other hand, if you weigh more than 180 pounds, you'll probably like the ride of an aluminum bike with oversize tubing. If you are in between those two weights, you can choose either type. Frame size also influences feel; a 25-inch frame is less rigid than a 19-inch frame made from the same tubing. Longer tubes flex more than shorter tubes.

David Barnes

Bill Davidson of Seattle, one of America's premier frame builders, produces limited-production and made-to-measure steel frames and complete bicycles.

For the wave of the future in pro bikes look to the raw materials and finished product of the Kestrel frame, made from molded carbon fiber (about $1,200, frame only).

Aluminum's strong points are that it's relatively inexpensive (it costs about the same as steel tubing), it's strong, it's highly corrosion-resistant, lightweight, and highly shock-absorbent. Aluminum tubing can be made more rigid than steel tubing of the same weight by altering the tube diameter or wall thickness. On the other hand, aluminum has a lower fatigue limit than steel tubing.

Composite—This term refers to bicycle frames whose tubing is made from layers of fiber and resin (glue). The most popular material is carbon fiber, but a composite frame may include many types of material—glass, graphite, or Kevlar. Recently, a revolutionary bicycle frame called the Kestrel has been made, not from carbon fiber tubing but as a single, molded carbon fiber unit. Designed by computer, carbon fiber technology is very expensive. On the positive side, carbon fiber frames are extremely strong, light, rigid, and fatigue-resistant. Depending on how the tubing is layered, carbon fiber bikes vary in their riding qualities.

Carbon fiber frames sell for $900 and up; a complete bicycle can range in price from $1800 to around $3000. Many riders find that most of the carbon fiber frames currently being produced ride very much like standard-diameter aluminum frames; they're shock-absorbent, while more rigid in the bottom bracket and a bit lighter than aluminum frames.

Titanium—At this writing, only one manufacturer, Fuji, is producing a bicycle with a titanium frame—and it costs $2500. Titanium tubing is much more expensive, much stronger, far more fatigue-resistant, far more corrosion-resistant, much lighter, and less rigid than steel tubing. More titanium frames will undoubtedly appear, but as is the case with composite frames, you can expect to see them only on high-end bicycles for a number of years.

It's possible to make a frame from aluminum tubing that's lighter and more rigid than a comparable steel frame. The potential for carbon fiber and titanium frames is even greater. Aluminum frames are currently comparable in price to steel frames; composite and titanium frames cost nearly twice as much as hand-built, custom steel frames and are likely to remain so for the next three to five years.

Scarpetta

BICYCLE COMPONENTS

A bicycle's components include everything attached to the frame—derailleurs, wheels, pedals, shift levers, brakes, hubs, a headset, saddle, handlebars, and so on. Most of the components found on quality bicycles, no matter what the brand, are made by one of the three companies—Shimano and SunTour of Japan, or Campagnolo of Italy. The biggest development in recent years, of course, has been indexed shifting, which refers to a gear-changing system pioneered by Shimano in 1985 in its high-end Dura-Ace component line for road bicycles.

The purpose of indexed shifting is to eliminate missed or imprecise shifts, drivetrain clatter, and the need to "fine tune" the shift after it has been made. The heart of indexed shifting is the shift lever for the rear derailleur, which moves through a series of precise stops, each one accompanied by a "click," and each corresponding to the exact location of a particular gear. Just pull back or push forward on the shift lever until you hear (and feel) a "click," and the rear derailleur moves the chain precisely up or down one gear. Perfection—no muss, no fuss.

In 1986, Shimano introduced indexed shifting (their system is known as SIS, for Shimano Index System) into its lower-priced 600EX and Light Action component groups. By late 1986, SunTour had introduced an indexed shifting system, as had Campagnolo (Syncro) and Huret (ARIS). For 1987, Shimano and SunTour extended indexed shifting to mountain bikes and into their lowest-priced component groups. Indexed shifting systems have proven themselves—they're easy to use, reliable, rarely go out of adjustment, and are easy to maintain.

Upward of 90 percent of racing, sport, and mountain bikes priced above $300 now have indexed shifting. Indexed shifting has become phenomenally popular, even among experienced cyclists who don't "need" it. Experienced riders find that indexed shifting helps them get the right shift easily when they're tired, or when they need to shift under pedaling load. Once cyclists try indexed shifting, very few turn the lever back to the optional "friction" mode. In fact, the motto in many a bike shop is, if it doesn't click, it doesn't sell.

But indexed shifting is only the most obvious example of a series of revolutionary changes in bicycle components in the last five years. A decade ago, only expensive bicycles had lightweight, attractive, reliable, and precise components—usually racing components made by Campagnolo. That's no longer the case. Campagnolo still produces high-end components and has introduced two component groups for mid-priced bicycles. But in the early 1980s, Shimano and SunTour took the initiative, producing attractive, high-quality, less expensive component groups for mid-priced bikes. (A component group is a complete set of components styled and designed to work together, and usually includes at least brake calipers and levers, front and rear derailleurs, shift levers, hubs, pedals, and a crankset).

Now, bicycles priced just above entry-level come equipped with well-made component groups. The components on today's low-and mid-priced bicycles, in fact, are far better than those found on the same level of bicycle in 1980; their quality comes much closer to that of expensive bicycles of the time. What's more, component quality has been improved across the board—riders notice the improved precision and feel of brakes and derailleurs, of course, but almost all components have been made more attractive, efficient, durable, and "user-friendly." The smoothness of bearings has been improved; components are more highly polished; pedals, brake, and shift levers have been ergonomically designed to work more efficiently and to fit the rider's hands and feet better; sealed cartridge bearings and O-ring seals make maintenance easier.

Shimano's top-of-the-line Dura-Ace group, the components which started the click-shift revolution in 1985. In 1987, new features included 7-speed shifting and aero brake levers. Dura-Ace is finding acceptance among many professional and amateur racers, as well as among fitness and recreational riders who ride high-end racing and triathlon bikes.

Gary Marcus/Shimano America

Joe McNally/Wheeler Pictures

Your choice of wheels and tires should be determined by your body weight and riding style.

OTHER CONSIDERATIONS

There are two other considerations to take into account when buying a new bike, both of which are component-related:

Wheels—Once you've bought the right size and type of frame for your riding needs, the next most important consideration is wheels. On production-line bicycles, wheel quality is pretty much matched to the type and quality of the frame and the other components. But keep in mind that light, narrow rims and tires will make a bike feel more responsive than medium-weight rims and wider tires; so if you find two bicycles that are comparable to one another in all respects except the wheels, that might be a deciding factor.

This doesn't mean that you should automatically choose the bike with high-performance wheels. First, consider your body weight, where you'll be riding the bike, and your level of cycling experience. If you weigh 200 pounds, you might decide that heavier rims and larger-section tires are a good idea because they'll be more comfortable and require truing less frequently. If you ride on streets that are full of potholes, choose a bike with sturdier wheels. Experienced riders know techniques that help their body, not their wheels, absorb shock. Beginners should choose durability over lightness until they master these techniques. Lightweight wheels are more fun to ride on, but they're not for everybody. If you decide to go with lighter wheels, make up your mind to take care of them by riding carefully and by regularly checking their trueness and spoke tension.

Gearing—Be sure that your new bike is geared appropriately to both the terrain you'll be riding on and your fitness level. Most racing and sport bikes come with front chainrings with 52 and 42 teeth and freewheels with a range from 13 to 24 teeth, appropriate for racing cyclists and for moderately conditioned riders who plan to ride over flat and rolling terrain. If you're out of shape or plan to ride hills regularly, you might want to switch the freewheel cogs and, if necessary, the rear derailleur to "touring gears" (14-30 or 14-32); you might even want to change to a triple crankset with a 28-tooth small chainring.

Your concern should be to obtain the right low gears for climbing hills. If you struggle up the hills you ride in your lowest gear on your current bike, get lower gears on your new bike. When in doubt, choose a lower "bail-out" gear. When you get stronger, you can change to higher gears if you wish. If you plan to change the gearing on your bike, do it before your new bike leaves the shop. It's simple and inexpensive to change chainrings and freewheels, or even a rear derailleur. If you decide you need a triple crankset, however, that will cost considerably more.

Today midpriced components (shown: Shimano's 600EX crankset) are designed as elegantly, and finished as lustrously, as the expensive components of a decade ago.

Steve Broaddus

Steve Broaddus

Courtesy of Schwinn Bicycle Co.

PRICE RANGES

Here's what's available in racing, sport, and mountain bikes in various price ranges. As you read about bicycles in various categories, however, please keep two things in mind. First, the categories themselves are arbitrary, and there aren't clear and absolute distinctions between bicycles priced closely to one another. Second, the prices at which you'll be likely to find certain features in a bicycle are true for mid-1987. Still, the general distinctions between categories of bikes apply and hold true irrespective of the value of the dollar.

Under $300

It's possible to buy a bicycle for $250 or less, but it's not a good idea. For a little more money, you'll get a lot more bicycle. About $300 is the least you can spend and still get a bicycle that's both fun to ride and durable. If you want to understand the differences better, check out the bicycles in department or general sporting

A good entry-level sport/touring bike, Schwinn's Le Tour (about $300) is relatively light and responsive—a good value for someone getting back into cycling who wants to enjoy riding a bike without spending a lot of money.

goods shops before you look at entry-level bikes in a good bike shop.

To their credit, many bicycles costing about $250 have cleanly constructed frames with flashy paint jobs. Some will have adequate brakes and indexed shifting. The saddles may be reasonably comfortable.

Remember, though, that bicycles aren't high-profit items—if one bicycle costs $50-$100 less than another, there's a reason. Virtually *everything* on bikes costing less than $300 will be of lower quality than the parts of bikes costing even $50 more. The main tubes on the frame may be chrome-moly steel, but it's unlikely that they'll be butted; the rest of the frame tubing will be lower-grade steel. The tires and wheels will be heavier, the shift levers will often be mounted on the handlebar stem, the brakes will be equipped with "safety levers" (a real misnomer because they make it more difficult to stop safely), the seat post probably will be made of steel and won't be the micro-adjusting type, the bearings will be of lower quality, and the bike will have fewer alloy parts and will be heavier.

$300–$500

Bicycles in this price range are designed as entry-level bicycles for the first-time serious recreational rider, someone who may not ride more than once or twice a week, but who wants a fairly good bike. A bike that costs at least $300 has superior features to bikes costing less, features you'll notice both in terms of performance and reliability. The three main tubes of the frame (at least) will be made of butted, chrome-moly steel; the dropouts will be forged. Some—perhaps most—of the components will be of superior quality. Brakes will be very good to excellent; indexed shifting will be *de rigueur*. The rims typically will be narrower and lighter. The frames will have plenty of braze-on fittings (double water bottle mounts, cable guides, a pump peg, a chain hanger). Toe clips and straps, and perhaps a water bottle and cage, may be standard equipment.

Within the $300–$500 price range, you'll find real variety among the bicycles available. Sport bikes and mountain bikes are the most common types, but there are a few racing bikes, too. The distinction between a racing and a sport bike in this price range is somewhat arbitrary; generally, racing bikes will have chain stays and a wheelbase that are 1–2 centimeters (½ to ¾ inch) shorter, and a head tube angle that's a degree steeper than a sport bike. Also, racing bikes will have a narrower range of gears, which will be higher than the gears on sport bikes.

Bicycles with various types of aluminum frames also are available in this price range. For example, Cannondale offers an aluminum-frame racing bike for $430, a touring bike for $350, and a mountain bike for $450; Raleigh has four composite aluminum/steel sport bikes ranging in price from $335–$435; BMX Products (Mangusta) makes a sport bike whose three main tubes are aluminum for $395; and Guerciotti makes an aluminum racing bike for $495.

There's a noticeable change in quality once you approach the $450 price point. Below that price, most bicycles are equipped with a variety of components. Starting at about $450, bicycles begin to come equipped with complete component

Nishiki's Olympic 12 (about $375) is an excellent value for an entry-level sport bike. (Right) Shimano's 105 Series is one of the best entry-level component groups to come along in recent years.

In components, the more you pay, the better the materials, design, and finish. Shown: a "generic" platform pedal and a C-Record pedal from Campagnolo.

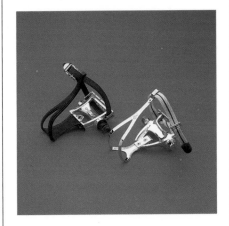

groups, most notably (on road bikes) the New 105 components from Shimano.

The New 105 component group was introduced in 1987 and is found on no fewer than twenty-five road bikes priced between $450–$600. New 105 components offer the casual recreational cyclist three significantly improved performance functions, apart from an attractive, integrated design: fast, precise "light touch" indexed shifting; computer-designed Biopace chainrings (their out-of-round design increases pedaling ease and efficiency through the power phase of the pedal stroke); and something not even higher-priced Shimano components have—SLR (Shimano Linear Response) brakes, which give a powerful, highly controllable braking response, plus a new, lighter feeling at the lever. This new component group is so good that *Bicycle Guide* magazine stated it offered customers "about 98 percent of all the performance that a group of

any price can offer." Other components you're likely to find in this price range are SunTour Alpha-5000 indexed shifting systems and (at the upper end) components from the Campagnolo Triomphe group.

There are more than fifty models of mountain bike priced between $300 and $500; better bikes come equipped with the well-regarded Shimano Deore or SunTour XC-Sport 7000 series indexed shifting systems, plus Shimano Deore or SunTour XC-Sport brakes. In this price range, most mountain bikes use Shimano Biopace, Sugino Cycloid, or SR SXC Ovaltech triple cranksets. The components (crankarms, stems, handlebars) on mountain and road bikes in the $300-$500 price range are sized in relation to the frame size, and the frames are typically sized in 2-inch (5-centimeter) increments (for example, 19, 21, 23, 25 and 27 inches).

Road bikes in this price range are fairly light (24 to 26 pounds), reliable, and easy to ride. They're stable and

inclined to go in a straight line, so that first-time adult riders will feel confident on them. Most low-priced ($300) mountain bikes, however, aren't really suitable for much more than casual cruising down hard-packed dirt roads; the components on these bikes aren't as rugged as those on mountain bikes priced closer to $500. Pedals and tires, in particular, aren't suited for heavy-duty hill climbing and descending on widely varying trail conditions. A bike such as the Specialized Rockhopper ($485), on the other hand, is a true mountain bike, and is generally considered to be one of the best values in an off-road bike at any price.

(Top and near right) The Nishiki Cascade and Specialized Rockhopper entry-level mountain bikes are genuine all-terrain bikes, capable of dependable service anywhere. Both cost about $500.

Courtesy of Specialized Bicycle Components

As you move from $300 to $500, the frames on both road bikes and mountain bikes improve, as do the components, in both aesthetic and functional terms. The quality of the frame tubing is better on $500 bikes, as is the finish work and paint job; the components are stronger, more precise, more durable, and more highly polished. And, since most of the components are aluminum alloy, nothing much will rust. More expensive bicycles in this price range are more likely to have sealing mechanisms against dirt and water in the four main bearing areas—hubs, pedals, headset, and bottom bracket. The wheels on a $500 bike will also be lighter, and the bike will be more responsive to ride.

In this price range particularly, bicycles priced closely to one another don't differ very much in terms of quality. Even brand names aren't very important. Although most experts agree that Japanese and American bicycles in this price range have the edge in quality, you can't discount bikes from Taiwan (for example, the Specialized Rockhopper mentioned above) or Europe. Most frames found on $300–$500 bikes are made in essentially the same way; so relax, find a good bike shop (more about that in the next chapter), and be confident that you're spending enough money to get a quality bicycle.

(Below) Contemporary mountain bike componentry. Top to bottom: SunTour XC Sport roller cam brakes; Shimano's Deore U-Brake; SunTour's XC Sport 7000 rear derailleur.

Steve Broaddus

$500–$800

Bicycles in the $300–$500 price range are for casual recreational cyclists who appreciate a lightweight, relatively responsive bicycle; bicycles in the $500–$800 price range are intended for cyclists who plan to use a bike for fitness training, centuries (100-mile or 160-kilometer rides) and competitive riding (triathlons and bike racing). These bikes are designed to be more lightweight, more responsive, and more durable than $300–$500 bicycles.

As you would expect, performance quality goes up on $500–$800 bicycles—but not in direct relation to the increase in price. That is, a $700 bicycle is not going to perform 100 percent better than a $350 bicycle. It's hard to put the actual improvement in quantitative terms, but it's probably closer to 25 percent. (The important components on a $700 bike might last twice as long as those on a $350 bike, however.) This rule—as the price increases, the percentage of improvement in performance diminishes—applies even more rigorously as bicycles become more expensive.

In this price range, all bicycles are still *production bikes*; they come mass-produced from the manufacturer as complete bicycles. They're often available in more sizes (2-centimeter rather than 2-inch increments) than lower-priced bikes, you can usually choose from one of two colors, and you can modify some components on the bike without paying extra for labor. The frames on these bikes are typically good enough to consider upgrading the components at some point.

Bikes that cost between $500 and $800 feel different to ride from the way less expensive bikes feel. To the novice rider, they will probably feel a little unstable. Actually, the opposite is true. Typically, bikes in this price range have slightly shorter wheelbases, slightly less fork rake, and slightly steeper head tube angles than less expensive bikes designed for the same purpose, which makes them more *responsive*. That means that they respond more accurately to small changes in steering input, so they require more skill to ride well. Less expensive bikes feel awkward and unwieldy if you try to ride fast or take corners hard with them—it's the difference between driving a station wagon and a sports car.

As bicycles become more expensive, they seem (to the inexperienced rider) skittish at low speeds. Don't worry about these handling differences, though; if you're interested in riding a bike frequently for fitness training or for riding long distances (50 miles [80 Kilometers]), you'll quickly get used to (and appreciate) a more responsive bicycle.

Most of the frames in this price range are still made from high-quality chrome-moly steel. Name-brand tubing is the rule in these bikes—Tange Champion and Columbus SL are the most common in road bikes, with Tange MTB most commonly used for mountain bikes. Aluminum frames comprise about 10 percent of the total, but will undoubtedly become more popular in the future.

Again, component quality goes up and weight goes down in this category, mostly because of lighter wheels

(Left) Univega's Alpina Pro (about $600); (below) Shimano's 600EX components, found on most new midpriced sport bikes.

Univega

Steve Broaddus

Steve Broaddus

(built with lighter rims, and often only 32 spokes instead of 36). Racing bikes weigh from 21 to 23 pounds, sport bikes typically weigh between 22 and 25 pounds, and mountain bikes average about 28 pounds, two pounds less than $300–$500 mountain bikes.

Components in this price range are more precise and durable. Manufacturers use more of such design features as Teflon™ bushings, lined cable housing, and oversize cables to reduce friction and improve braking performance. Derailleur parts are made from harder metals and their fit is more precise, improving durability. There's more attention to sealing the bearings against dirt and water than there is on lower-priced components. Manufacturers design mid-range components to hold up and perform well under harder and more competitive use than most recreational cyclists subject their bikes to. Also, the finish on all the components in this price range is better, including the

seat post, stem, and handlebars.

Shimano's excellent 600EX components dominate the road bikes in this category; there's also a sprinkling of Shimano Sante and 105 components, along with representation from the SunTour Cyclone 7000, Sprint 9000, and the Campagnolo Victory component groups. Among the high-quality rims available on $500–$800 bikes are Araya 20-A, Mavic MA-40, Araya SS-40, and Ambrosio Elite Durex models.

The trend in mountain bikes is similar to that in road bikes—those in the $500–$800 price category are somewhat lighter and more performance-oriented. The big news in mountain bike components is the introduction in 1987 of the completely new Deore XT group, which many off-road riders consider to be the mountain bike equivalent of Shimano's top-of-the-line Dura-Ace road bike components.

The Deore XT group features a highly polished, forged triple crankset equipped with Biopace II chain rings; a superb braking system consis-

ting of redesigned brake levers, cantilever (front) and U-brake (rear) calipers; SIS shift levers and rear derailleur; a front derailleur; hubs; pedals; a seat-post quick-release lever; and a chain deflector. Everything works better than previous Shimano components, which were already the best available; the new Deore XT components have established themselves as the state-of-the-art mountain bike group.

There's more good news—you'll only have to spend about $650 to get a mountain bike equipped with the complete group (compared to at least $1100 for a road bike with top-of-the-line components). But for those who can't or don't want to spend that kind of money, Deore XT-like performance is available in $500–$600 bikes equipped with Deore components—the finish of the components isn't the same quality as that of the Deore XT, but the design and most of the working parts are. (Unfortunately, Deore components only include brakes,

Steve Broaddus

shifters, and derailleurs, not the full group.)

Also, the wheels on mountain bikes in this category are lighter, thanks to the use of high-quality rims such as the Araya RM-20, which weigh about eight ounces less than the Araya 7X, commonly used on less expensive mountain bikes.

As you can see, bicycles in the $500–$800 price category are intended for frequent, hard use, rather than the infrequent, casual use $300–$500 bicycles receive. A bicycle in the $500–$800 price range will feel lighter, more precise, and more responsive than a less expensive bike; it will be more exciting to ride. The frame and components will be better finished, more reliable, and durable than less expensive ones. In this price range, you'll get 90 percent of the performance of the best bicycles available for half the cost.

Two of the most popular sport bikes offer instructive examples of what makes one bike cost more than another. Centurion now makes two models of their top-selling triathlon bike, the Dave Scott Ironman. The lower-priced model is called the Ironman Expert; its frame is constructed from a custom mix of Tange Champion No. 1 double-butted chrome-moly steel alloy tubing, and it uses Shimano's New 105 components. The Ironman Expert has a suggested retail price (early 1987) of $550.

The Ironman Master, on the other hand, has essentially the same frame, rims, tires, stem, and handlebars, but it has a better saddle and, more important, is equipped with Shimano's 600EX components, which are more highly polished, use higher-quality materials, and are made with more expensive production methods. The price of the Ironman Master, therefore, is higher—$680.

So, how much should you spend? The harder you ride your bike—and the more you like the feeling of fine machinery—the more you should be willing to pay.

(Left) A midpriced solution for small riders is the Centurion "Dave Scott Ironman" (about $575) with a 24-inch front wheel. (Below) Schwinn's Circuit (about $700) features Columbus tubing in the frame and SunTour's Sprint components.

$800 and Up

If you're a rapidly improving cyclist with a taste for the finest equipment, you may be interested in bicycles costing $800 and up, sometimes referred to as "pro" bikes. Pro bikes are flashy, fast, and exotic, the two-wheeled equivalent of a Porsche or Lamborghini. If you're considering buying a bicycle in this price range, however, keep in mind that to some degree you're dealing with "jewelry," meaning that you're not necessarily concerned only with function; you're moving into the realm of *wants* as much as *needs*. Put another way, one of the principal appeals of the pro bike is *passion*. Sure, pro bikes perform, but compared to less expensive bikes, there's far less relation between an increase in price and an increase in performance.

Let's get a few things straight—we're talking about a category of bikes that starts at $800 and extends to $3000 or more. Most of the available models (67 percent, or 100 out of 150) are high-end road-racing bikes. What do you get for your money?

You *do* get function. The compo-

nents on these bikes, for example, are absolutely the best available. They're designed from the best materials to be as strong as possible, to withstand the rigors (and abuses) of professional bicycle racing. They're constructed without compromise to the most exacting mechanical tolerances, by means of the most costly manufacturing processes, so that they work flawlessly over and over again under any load and climate conditions they may encounter.

These components are so well-made that the average consumer gets a product requiring almost no maintenance at all. Campagnolo used to be the preeminent force in racing components, but that's no longer the case. The best component groups in this category are Shimano's Dura-Ace, Campagnolo's C-Record and Super Record, and SunTour's Superbe Pro. All offer excellent performance and reliability; which component group you prefer is as much a matter of personal preference as anything else. Talk to a lot of experienced riders, and try out the components you're interested in before you buy.

On bikes of this caliber, the "pas-

When you spend $800 or more, you get the best components available. (Top) Campagnolo's new Chorus line (no pun intended) and SunTour's Superbe Pro racing rear derailleur.

Cycle Composites' carbon fiber Kestrel, equipped with Campagnolo's C-Record components.

Scarpetta

sive" components (those with no moving parts) are also top-notch. The handlebars, stem, saddle, seat post, rims, and spokes are designed to be light, strong, corrosion-resistant, attractive, and well-finished.

In the pro bike category, you also get the latest high-tech developments first, especially in terms of the "ultimate" frame technology. Currently, that would be composite frames, mostly some type of carbon fiber/Kevlar combination. If you can't live without the most recent "wonderbike," though, you'll pay for it—for example, the cheapest complete bikes with carbon fiber frames cost about $1800.

Being the first on your block with new-bike goodies has its advantages and disadvantages. On one hand, you get to enjoy them *right away* (a temporary cure for some forms of Severe Bike Lust), and often the cost of the high-tech features you've bought won't trickle down to lower-priced gear for years. On the other hand, you run the risk of paying a high price for cycling gear that doesn't live up to its advance billing.

Another reason to buy a pro bike is that you appreciate fine craftsmanship; if you pay enough money for a frame builder's labor and materials, you can get whatever strikes your fancy in terms of exotic metalwork and paint jobs, as well as custom-engraved components. But the advantages of the superior craftsmanship in a pro frameset extend beyond the merely decorative. If you buy a frame from a builder with a good reputation, it will be made more carefully and precisely than a mass-produced frame constructed from the same tubing. It will be stronger, aligned better, and the finish work and paint will be of a higher quality.

Finally, let's not overlook *status*, a prime reason that many cyclists purchase pro bikes. It may not be the best reason to buy an expensive bike, but if you're going to spend a thousand dollars or more for a bicycle, you might as well be honest about the reasons.

Scarpetta

If you want to be extravagant, cycling gives you the opportunity with the limited-edition Maruishi carbon fiber frame outfitted with gold-plated Campagnolo components.

Vic Huber Photography

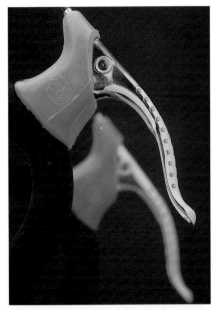

Vic Huber Photography

Vic Huber Photography

Vic Huber Photography

To sum up, pro bikes ($800 and up) feel more responsive, more lively and more precise than mid-priced ($500–$800) bikes, though you'll pay twice as much or more than you'd pay for a mid-priced bike in order to get 10 percent more performance. (You *will* get a lot more long-term durability and reliability with a pro bike, however.)

It may be worth it to you to buy a pro bike—if you think so, take a few for test rides and honestly evaluate whether you can tell the difference between them and bikes costing half as much. Rely on your own experience and the advice of experienced cyclists you trust to decide whether any bike is worth the purchase price. Remember, just because you can afford a high-priced bike doesn't guarantee you'll enjoy riding it.

So far, most of the discussion has been about expensive road bikes. The fact of the matter is, there are more than forty mountain bikes available that cost more than $800. What do you

get for your money in a high-end mountain bike?

You get top-of-the-line components, of course, but you can get those on a $750 mountain bike, too. What you get on an expensive mountain bike is one or more of the following: superb hand-craftsmanship, custom graphics, exotic materials (aluminum), and an extremely rugged or special-purpose frame (for example, for expedition touring or observed trials). Most people probably can get by just fine on a production-line mountain bike—but then, the same could be said about road bikes.

If you decide you want to buy a pro bike, you have several options:

Expensive production bikes—Most well-known bike manufacturers offer high-quality bicycles that you can buy off the floor or special-order from your bike shop. Examples of this type of bike are the Univega Superstrada, Cannondale SR2000, Nishiki Carbon/Kevlar, Trek 2000, and Specialized Team Allez.

High performance on a "budget"—the Univega Superstrada (below, about $1,200) and Specialized Team Allez (right, about $1,500).

Univega

(Left) Shimano's Deore XT cantilevers, the best in mountain bike brakes, grace a Tom Ritchey frame.

Steve Broaddus

Courtesy of Specialized Bicycle Components

The advantages of buying this type of bike are that the frames are carefully produced (either hand-made or on a limited-production basis) and equipped with top-of-the-line components; therefore, you can often get a high-quality bike with high-tech features at a relatively low price. You can also test-ride the bike before you buy it to see if you like it. A disadvantage is that many of these bikes come with tubular rims and tires as standard equipment, which you may not want (see below).

Limited-production bikes—This refers to complete bicycles hand-made on a limited basis by established frame builders such as Bruce Gordon, Bill Davidson, Ben Serotta, Dave Moulton, Richard Sachs, and Tom Kellogg. These bikes may be a little more expensive than the production bikes mentioned above, but they're likely to be made more carefully, and you may have a greater choice of color or components. Buying a bike this way is more complicated (it may involve traveling to another city to find a dealer in order to test-ride a bike, place an order, and so on), but it might be worth it to get the bike you want.

Made-to-measure bikes—These are similar to the limited-production bikes, except that the frame is tailored to your individual body measurements and riding style. This option is more expensive, but gives you more choices. If you're especially short or tall or otherwise hard to fit, it may be the best course of action. Good bike shops often sell frames made by custom builders or can put you in touch with one.

Building up a bike from a frameset—Most quality bike shops sell bare framesets ready to be built up into pro bikes; these frame sets can cost from $400 to $1000 and more. Such framesets are made from all types of materials, in all sorts of configurations (racing, mountain, touring). You can choose the frame and components you want, have the shop build you a set of wheels, assemble the bike, and fit you to it—all according to your requirements. Again, by buying a bike this way, you maximize your choices.

Speaking of choices, if you buy a pro bike, you'll also have to choose the type of wheels and tires you want. Your body weight and riding style will

Superb craftsmanship and meticulous attention to detail characterize framesets by master frame builders, such as this one from Bill Davidson.

Vic Huber Photography

Vic Huber Photography

play a large role in determining how light your rims, spokes, and tires can be, and how many spokes you'll want to use. You'll also have to decide whether you want to specify clincher or tubular tires. To help you figure out which you want, ask yourself these questions: Do you enjoy tinkering with your bike? Are you willing to spend considerably more money on tires for a slight gain in performance? Are you willing to tolerate more flats?

The fact is, tubular tires feel wonderful to ride, but they're also expensive, messy to glue on a rim, and difficult to repair. If you plan to compete seriously in triathlons or bike races, you might consider buying two sets of wheels—clinchers to train on and tubulars to compete with. Otherwise, you'll probably be perfectly happy using high-pressure clinchers for all your cycling.

PITFALLS TO AVOID

When you start shopping for a pro bike, don't let anybody talk you into believing that one particular brand of frame or component group is "*the* hot ticket," and that all others are inferior. For example, there's still a prevalent belief that Italian frames and components perform better than any others, which is mostly a result of the mystique surrounding European racing.

Don't get taken in by this myth or any other. Trust your own experience, and talk to people who know more than you do. Read books and magazines about cycling. Most of all, be absolutely clear what criteria are important to you in a bike, and don't let anyone talk you into buying anything else. Ride a variety of bikes before you buy one—everything from a mid-priced triathlon bike to an ultraexpensive criterium machine. Decide for yourself whether you want a steel, aluminum, or carbon fiber frame; tubular or clincher wheels; Shimano, Campagnolo, or Sun Tour components.

For more information on the range of what's available, consult the experts at your local pro bike shop, as well as the buyer's guide issue of *Bicycling, Cyclist,* or *Bicycle Guide* magazines, which come out every spring. Each lists the prices and technical specifications for hundreds of bicycles.

There's no point in spending $1800 on a bike you find you don't like.

(Above) Although it may look strange, Nishiki's Fusion bike (about $1,100) is perfect for time trials and triathlons. (Left) Rear disc wheels are more efficient, resulting in faster times.

Scarpetta

Don Lauritzen/Courtesy of Nishiki Bicycle Co.

How To Buy A Bicycle

At this point, you've taken a good, hard look at yourself and determined what you want in a bicycle: you're familiar with the types of bikes available, and you have a general idea of the features you'll find in everything from entry-level to pro bikes. Now we come to the part you've been waiting for—actually buying your bike.

CHOOSING THE RIGHT BIKE SHOP

The most important decision you'll make about your bike and related cycling equipment is where to buy it, so the first step is choosing the right shop. This is true for a number of reasons. First, as mentioned in the last chapter, deciding the type and quality level of bike you want to buy is more important than the various brands available. At any quality level, brands differ from one another far less than the quality of shops selling those bicycles.

Second, the knowledgeable people at a good bike shop will give you sound advice about the best bike and cycling equipment for your needs, make sure the bike you want to buy fits you properly, and adjust it correctly for you. The shop's mechanics will assemble your bike, make any modifications necessary to customize it, and usually offer a free, thirty-day tune-up; the bike shop also plays an integral role in follow-up service and maintenance.

Owners of good bike shops value the interested cyclist, because they have a real service to provide and know that they have to treat customers fairly or risk losing their business and the business of friends they might refer to the shop. Bike shops, unlike car dealerships, don't make a lot of profit on sales—they rely on return

business for service, clothing, and accessories. When you've found a shop you can trust, you'll discover that it's a good source of information not only for bikes and accessories, but for cycling activities as well. Shops often sponsor group rides, for example, as well as maintenance and repair clinics.

The best way to find a good bike shop is to ask other cyclists for their recommendations. Find out which shops racers, triathletes, and serious recreational cyclists patronize. If you

don't know any cyclists, pick up the Yellow Pages and find listings for shops that specialize in high-end equipment, racing bikes, and cycling clothing. (You can sometimes recognize these shops from the difficult-to-pronounce names of the bikes they sell—CIÖCC, Maruishi, 3 Rensho, Vitus, and so on.)

If you're looking for a relatively inexpensive bike however, you may find a greater selection, and more personal attention in a shop that caters to family cycling.

Steve Broaddus

Tom Raymond / Fresh Air Photographics

The sales people at a good bike shop will explain the available options. (Left) Mark Sorbello of the MDR Bike Shop in Marina Del Rey, California, demonstrates the difference between a woman's and man's saddle to Alice Mendoza, who rides for fun and fitness. (Above) Checking out the latest cycling equipment and accessories.

So, spend the first few hours that you devote to buying a bike by visiting different bike shops, picking up product literature, and talking briefly to sales people. The first time you visit a shop, though, spend most of your time watching and listening to what goes on. Pay attention to the way a shop treats other customers. If you've heard good things about a shop, give it a fair chance—everybody has bad days, but a shop with a good word-of-mouth reputation usually deserves it.

Here are some indications that a shop will do a good job of satisfying your needs:

1. *The shop has a good selection of the type of bicycle you want to buy, ranging from entry-level to high-end bikes.* Also, the shop should have a salesperson who can knowledgeably discuss these bikes with you. If you're a novice, how can you tell? Trust your instincts—in a good bike shop, salespeople will be enthusiastic and helpful, listening patiently and carefully to customers' questions but not trying to pressure them to buy a particular kind of bike or piece of cycling equipment. If a salesperson makes a statement, he or she should be able to support it. Don't be afraid to ask for more information.

2. *A shop's style should fit yours.* If you're interested in touring or recreational cycling, you might not feel comfortable in a shop that caters mostly to the hard-core racing crowd. A shop may have the best mechanics or the most technically competent sales staff, but if the people there aren't interested in the way you want to use your bicycle, the shop will be pretty useless to you. On the other hand, a particular shop may not have the best selection or prices, but if the staff seems interested in your kind of cycling, get to know them better.

Of course, "style" means something other than an approach to riding. Perhaps you prefer a shop where the employees will take a lot of time discussing bike information with you, rather than expecting you to know exactly what you want when you come in. If so, find a shop where the salespeople take this approach. (In fairness to bike shops and their employees, you should be aware that most good shops are jammed during the peak cycling months of April through September—especially on weekends—and be sensitive to the fact that employees simply won't have as much time to discuss bicycle minutiae as they'd like.)

3. *The shop should have skilled personnel to assemble and maintain the bicycles it sells.* Production bicycles arrive at a dealer partially assembled by the factory, but better shops always assume that factory assembly procedures are incomplete and that the bike must be gone over carefully. Examine the bikes lined up on the shop's floor to see that "extras"

have been attended to; spin the wheels to see whether they've been trued. Check for uniform spoke tension. Make sure that the cables have been lubricated and that the seat post, stem, and bolt threads have been greased. Check to see that the cable ends have been capped. Ask whether the shop's mechanics add grease to and adjust the bearings in the hubs, headset, pedals, and bottom bracket of the bikes during assembly. Find out if the shop checks frame and fork alignment. If a shop follows through on most of these procedures, it's a good indication that it will provide

quality service after the sale.

Finding a good bike shop takes work, but it's worth it. It will increase your enjoyment and enthusiasm for riding your new bike, because you'll feel confident that you have friends you can rely on to give you good advice and help you solve any cycling problems that arise.

Remember, you're not just buying a bicycle—you're looking for a complete package consisting of cycling expertise, a caring attitude, as well as a good selection of bicycles and equipment. Taken together, that's what makes up a bicycle purchase.

Steve Broaddus

(Right) A competent salesperson will be able to meaningfully compare the differences between the features on bicycles in different price categories.

Steve Broaddus

(Left) The shop you patronize should employ competent mechanics who can keep your bike in great repair.

GOING SHOPPING

Now that you've sized up a number of shops and narrowed your choice to one or two, it's time to do some serious bicycle shopping. Don't walk into a shop cold, however; call ahead to ask which employee specializes in the kind of bike you're interested in buying. Make an appointment when he or she is least busy and can spend up to an hour talking with you. Take the shoes and the shorts you ride in with you to the shop.

Many people who are new to cycling find bike shops intimidating, which is why it helps to do your homework. This *doesn't* mean that you have to be an expert in frame

geometry or the latest components. In fact, a good salesperson will appreciate it if you're candid about how much or how little you know about bicycles. He or she should be asking helpful questions (such as those mentioned in the first chapter), rather than trying to impress you with technical expertise. If the salesperson is astute, he will be talking to you at your level. If a salesperson uses technical jargon you don't understand, ask for a different salesperson. If you're prepared and the salesperson is competent, and if the shop has a good selection of bikes, it shouldn't take very long for you to narrow the number of appropriate bikes to two or three.

Getting the correct frame size
(above) is *the* first major step in
buying a bike. (Right) Can you find
at least two things wrong with this
picture?

OBTAINING THE CORRECT FRAME SIZE

When you first start looking, make sure that the bikes in which you're interested can be adjusted so that the saddle, bars, and pedals are efficiently and comfortably positioned.

If you've picked a good shop, the salespeople there probably know how to determine the right frame size for you. But points of view on correct bike-fit vary, and there's no reason to spend a lot of money on a bike that doesn't fit you properly. If it doesn't, you'll always be compensating in some way when you ride, and you'll never ride as comfortably or efficiently as you would on the right size bike.

Fit is paramount, because in cycling, as in no other sport, the equip- ment dictates technique. In running or swimming, for example, proper technique is achieved by changing the body's movements to achieve greater efficiency. A runner lowers his hands to waist level or shortens his stride, but a cyclist's movements are restricted by the relative positions of the bicycle's components. The bicycle must therefore be fitted correctly in order for a sound basis for proper technique to be established.

Some of the bicycle's components —the stem, handlebars, seat post, and pedals, for example—can easily be changed to accommodate differing body dimensions. In the chapter on bike fit, I'll discuss bike-fit criteria as they apply to components. The focus here, however, will be to help you understand how to determine correct frame size.

Most quality adult bicycles come in at least four frame sizes—19, 21, 23, and 25 inches (48, 53, 58, and 64 cen- timeters); moderately expensive bicy- cles are available in 2-centimeter or 1- inch increments; and expensive bicy- cles are constructed with seat tube lengths that vary by 1 centimeter. The majority of cyclists, however, can be fitted on the commonly available sizes.

Most fitting methods require that the rider initially straddle the bicycle to determine the clearance between the rider's crotch and the bike's top tube; one inch of clearance means that the frame fits correctly.

This method may be fine for male riders of average height, but it often doesn't work well for women (who typically have short torsos and long legs compared to men) and for shorter or taller riders. Correct strad- dle clearance also depends on riding style—a short touring rider might have virtually no straddle clearance, while a tall racer may have as much as three inches (eight centimeters).

THE IMPORTANCE OF STEM HEIGHT

When most riders think of adjusting their bikes, they think of modifying the *reach* (the distance from the seat to the handlebars, achieved by changing the stem length) or *leg extension* (raising or lowering the seat post). The range of adjustment of these components will accommodate a wide variation of body dimensions: Stems are available in sizes from 4 to 14 centimeters (a range of 3½ inches), and seat posts are available as long as 300 millimeters (12 inches).

There is one other important dimension, however, that has a direct bearing on your choice of frame size: *stem height*, which determines handlebar height, and therefore how upright or bent-over your position on the bike will be. Most high-quality stems can only be safely raised or lowered a maximum of 4 to 5 centimeters (1¾ to 2 inches). It's critical, then, to choose a frame size that allows you to adjust the handlebar height properly; everything else can be adjusted around that.

It's important not to pick a frame size that's too small. If you buy a frame that's too small, you'll have to compensate to get proper leg extension by raising your seat post, but you may not be able to raise your stem a corresponding amount to be comfortable, and you may wind up too bent over on your bike. This is fine for would-be bike racers (which is one of the reasons racers advocate choosing the smallest possible frame), but most people find it uncomfortable to ride with their backs nearly horizontal.

To find your correct frame size, first adjust the seat height on the bike you're considering buying until it feels about right; your leg should be almost fully extended at the bottom of the pedal stroke, and your hips should not rock back and forth on the saddle as you pedal. Then, raise the stem out of the head tube as high as it will safely go (look for the "minimum insertion" mark on the stem). Now look at the bike from the side and note the position of the handlebars in relation to the seat height. If you're buying a touring or sport bike, you should be able to adjust the stem vertically so that the handlebars are even with, or slightly below, the seat. For very tall riders the bars can be one to two inches (two to four centimeters) below the seat to allow a fairly upright torso position, which most people initially find comfortable. If you like to work hard and go fast, you'll want to lower the bars to decrease wind resistance and maximize power output. To achieve a more competitive position, move the bars an inch or two (two or four centimeters) below the seat for average-sized riders, and two or three inches (five or eight centimeters) below the seat for taller riders. Short riders should avoid any bike that won't allow the bars to be raised to the level of the saddle.

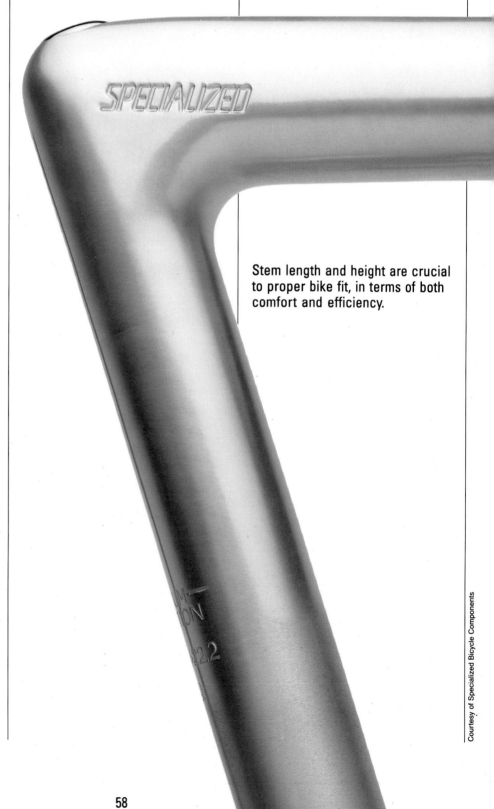

Stem length and height are crucial to proper bike fit, in terms of both comfort and efficiency.

Courtesy of Specialized Bicycle Components

If you buy a frame that's large enough, you'll be able to raise the handlebars to a height that allows a comfortable torso angle; you can always lower them if you want to ride more aggressively and efficiently, but you can't raise them any higher than the limit mark on the stem. Especially tall riders may need a special, extra-long stem for them to be comfortable.

Steve Broaddus

Imre J. Barsy

SPECIAL FITTING PROBLEMS

If you're in between frame sizes, you may want to rely on the length of the bicycle's top tube to determine which bike you buy. As a bike's seat tube gets longer, so does the top tube (although there is some variation among different brands of bikes). If you have a short torso and long legs (as do many women), pick the smaller frame if it has a shorter top tube so you won't be too stretched-out over the bike. Riders with long torsos and short legs may prefer a larger frame with a longer top tube. If you're in between sizes and the longer top tube won't cause you any problems, get the bigger bike; otherwise, the uncomfortably low bar position may give you a pain in the neck. Take a tape measure with you when you go shopping, and look for the bike that gives you the right combination of seat tube and top tube length for your body type.

Until recently, women have had problems buying bicycles that fit them well. Bikes have traditionally been designed *by* men to work well *for* men. A woman will probably be more comfortable, for example, on a frame with a top tube that's about one inch shorter than the top tube of a bike that would fit a man her height.

Women taller than five-feet-six-inches (1.68 meters) usually have no problems; they're able to compensate for a longer top tube by using a shorter stem. Small women have an even greater problem, because there's a limit to how short a stem can be used before it adversely affects bike handling, and there's a limit to how short top tube length can be cut before a standard, 27-inch (69-centimeter) front wheel interferes with toe-clip clearance.

A leading pioneer in the development of women's bicycles is a female frame builder, Georgena Terry, who designs and builds bicycles in her shop in East Rochester, New York. In the past two years, bicycle manufacturers have also responded to the fitting problems of shorter riders and women riders in two ways: to build bicycles with shorter top tubes in general and, in especially small sizes (18 inches [45 centimeters] and under) to build bikes with slightly sloping top tubes and/or small (24-inch [61-centimeter]) front wheels. In 1987, there were almost forty models of bicycles in all price ranges suited to smaller riders.

Really tall riders have problems with bike fit, too, but not because of inherent design problems—it's just that very few manufacturers (if any) make frames larger than 25 inches (64 centimeters). Tall riders may be forced to solve their problems by having frames custom-built to their specifications.

In addition to problems with frame size, tall and short riders have traditionally had problems obtaining components of the proper size—seat posts, pedals, toe clips, stems, crank arms, and handlebars. A greater selection of all of these components has become available in the past several years, however.

Steve Broaddus

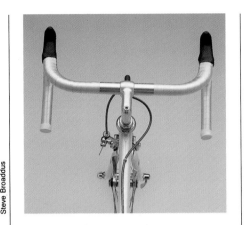

Steve Broaddus

Steve Broaddus

Steve Broaddus

For small riders afflicted with Severe Bike Lust, here is a top-of-the-line Georgena Terry frameset decked out with Shimano Dura-Ace components.

Steve Broaddus

TAKING A TEST RIDE

When you've found several bikes that you like and that fit you, it's time to do some test riding. A good shop will not only allow you to take a bike for a test ride, they'll insist on it. If a shop refuses your request to test ride a bike you like, go somewhere else.

What you should expect from a test ride depends on the type of bike you're considering and your cycling experience. It's very difficult, for instance, to tell much about how a mountain bike will perform off-road, if you only take it for a test ride on the streets near the bike shop. Similarly, if you're used to riding department-store ten-speeds, any good entry-level bike will feel good to ride.

Still, there are a number of things to look for that will indicate not only the quality of the bike, but the care that's gone into assembling and adjusting it. First, inspect the entire bike before riding it—try the brake levers to check for proper adjustment, make

sure the tires are inflated to the correct pressure, and check to see that the finish isn't scratched and is free of grease.

When you start riding, shift the bike through all the gears, riding in each for a short distance. The derailleurs and brakes should work smoothly and quietly—the sign of a well-adjusted bike. Take the bike through corners at varying speeds, never pushing it above what seems a safe and comfortable level. All bikes handle differently and take getting used to, but you should be able to tell right away whether you like the way a bike feels. Does it seem responsive and lively, or slow and sluggish? Is it stable, or does it seem skittish and unpredictable? Does it corner easily, as if it's on rails, or does it resist, requiring you to force it into a turn?

On a straightaway, stand up and, in a high gear, sprint hard down the street. Does the bike move easily under you? Does it feel rigid and efficient, transferring all your energy into forward motion? As you shift the bike from side to side while you're standing on

the pedals, there should be no unfamiliar squeaking or knocking from the bottom bracket area.

How about the components? Even on entry-level bikes today, the "working" components (brakes, shifters, and derailleurs) are designed well enough that they should function smoothly and precisely. When you're riding fairly fast, shift your weight to the rear of the saddle and check the brakes for effectiveness and smooth, controllable stopping power.

Of course, many factors contribute to a bike's "feel" and handling qualities—frame geometry and composition, wheel weight, tire size, component quality, and whether the bike is correctly adjusted to your body's dimensions. Ideally, a bike should feel like an extension of your body—never feel like it's fighting you as you pedal along.

You may need to go through this test-riding procedure at several shops to find the bike you like best. At each one, discuss the riding and handling qualities of the bikes you like with the salesperson to get a better under-

Steve Broaddus

standing of the reasons a bike responds in a given way. It's best to have this discussion *after* you ride the bike. Because the differences you can actually feel are small, the power of suggestion is very strong—if you discuss a bike's handling qualities before you ride it, it's likely that you'll think it rides the way the salesperson says it will. Keep lists—write down all the features you want in a bike and look for them. Try several bikes, and when you find the one you like best, try it again before you buy it.

The truth of the matter is, most good bikes of the same type will feel pretty similar. So how should you decide which one to buy? If you've done a good job of narrowing your choices, it doesn't matter. The quality will be nearly equal on all of them, so you can make your selection—with confidence—based on the fact that you like the color scheme of one bike or the aero brake levers on another.

It would be a mistake to ignore the emotional dimension of buying a bike. Choosing the bike you like is certainly a decision that involves passion and feelings; as you stand in the shop looking at a bike you like, it's natural to imagine yourself riding fast down a road, sweeping around corners. But take care of the rational aspects of buying a bicycle before you let a flashy paint job turn your brain to mush. Then you can buy a bike because you like its looks and still be assured that you got good value for your money.

Check the bike over thoroughly before you start the test ride. Make sure the shifters work properly (right) and that the bike feels light and agile during a standing sprint (left).

Steve Broaddus

CUSTOMIZING YOUR BIKE

When you finally buy your new bike, there are a few modifications you may need to make so that it suits your needs exactly, and it's best to make them before the bike leaves the shop. That's because the changes involve switching parts, and if you do it before you use the bike, you generally won't have to pay for the replacement parts or you'll only have to pay the difference in cost between them and the original equipment.

For instance, you might want to change:

1. The handlebar stem—To one that's longer, shorter, or higher, more suitable to your riding style.

2. The handlebars—When you're test-riding bikes, try ones with different shapes and widths of handlebars.

3. The pedals—If you have wide feet and the bike has quill pedals, they might be uncomfortably narrow. You might need to switch to platform or mountain bike pedals.

4. The seat post—Most good-quality bikes have microadjusting seat posts, which enable you to tilt your saddle at any angle you wish. If you're buying an entry-level bike, be sure it's equipped with one. Also, if you're tall or have long legs, be sure that the seat post is long enough.

5. The axles—Again, almost all quality bikes (but not some mountain bikes) have quick-release skewers and hollow axles on both wheels, which are a tremendous convenience in removing the wheels. It's worth the slight extra expense not to have to carry an axle-nut wrench with you all the time.

6. The tires—The issue here is size, not whether tires are treaded or treadless. If you're a large rider, riding on narrow (designated 20c or 25c) tires is going to be relatively uncomfortable compared to riding on tires with a larger cross-section (28c or 32c). You'll get fewer flats on larger tires, too.

7. The gearing—Depending on your strength and the terrain you ride, you may need lower gears. Talk to your salesperson—it's possible to

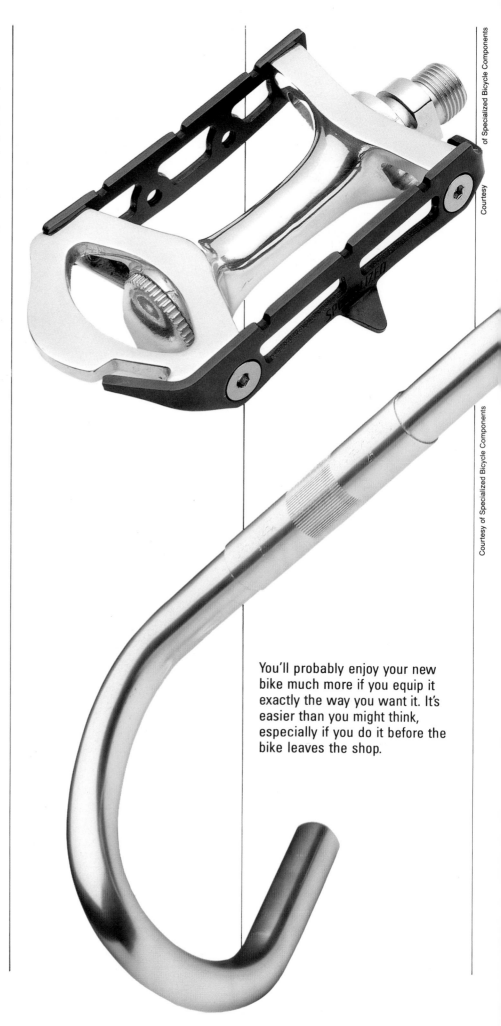

You'll probably enjoy your new bike much more if you equip it exactly the way you want it. It's easier than you might think, especially if you do it before the bike leaves the shop.

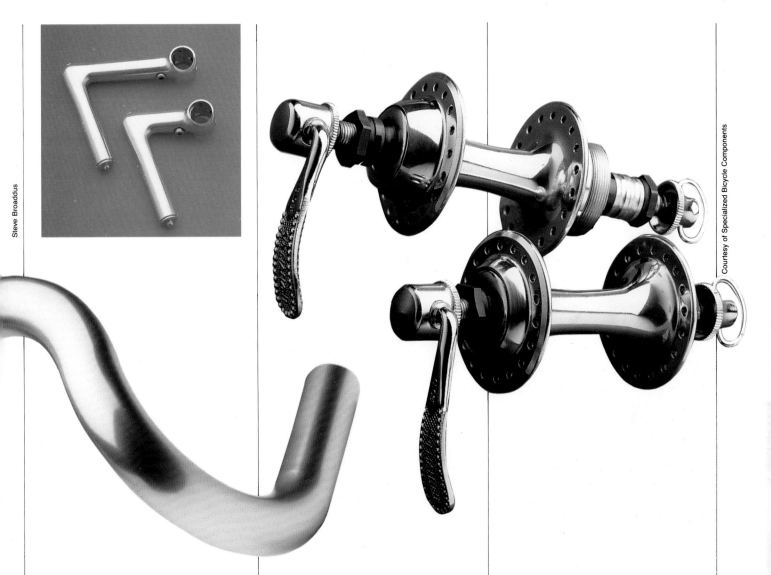

Steve Broaddus

Courtesy of Specialized Bicycle Components

switch to larger freewheel cogs or smaller chainrings.

8. The crank arms—Quality bikes have components that are proportionately sized, but if you have especially long or short legs, you may want to change the length of the crank arms, although the cost usually outweighs the benefits.

9. The saddle—This component is crucial to your riding comfort, and there's no easy way to determine which saddle is best for you. Some rear-end soreness is inevitable for those just beginning cycling after a long layoff, or dramatically increasing their mileage or their riding frequency. But if the pain persists for more than a few weeks, you probably need a different saddle.

In general, women need wider saddles because of their wider pelvic structure. Fortunately, plenty of options have been developed in the last few years to maximize comfort for both men and women; good bike shops will let you try several saddles so that you can find the one that fits your anatomy best. For a more extensive discussion of how to choose a comfortable saddle, see the chapter on "cycling tips."

10. Handlebar tape, toe straps, pumps, saddle covers—All come in many colors, so feel free to make an aesthetic statement with your bike. Padded handlebar coverings are great for entry-level or touring cyclists.

Customers shopping for a new bicycle typically have a different point of view about making changes to a bike than do the shop's employees. You might think it's asking too much to change a seat post or handlebar tape (especially if you're not sure how to do it yourself). The employees in a good shop, however, want to make customers happy. They're experienced in bike assembly, and since most bikes come only partially as-sembled from the factory anyway, they're very willing to accommodate a customer's wishes.

There's a line from a movie, *The Last Detail*, that fits well here. Jack Nicholson plays one of two military policemen taking a young sailor, played by Randy Quaid, to a military prison in another city. En route, the trio stops at a restaurant for what will be one of the sailor's last meals outside prison walls. The three men order cheeseburgers and malts; Quaid's comes back with the cheese unmelted. He admits that he'd really have preferred it melted, but he'll eat it the way it is. Nicholson grabs the burger and calls over the waiter. "Melt the cheese on this for the chief," he says, then turns to Quaid and looks him squarely in the face. "It's just as easy, Meadows," he says slowly, "to have it the way you want it."

The same applies to your new bike.

BEFORE YOU LEAVE THE SHOP

A good shop will have carefully assembled and adjusted your new bike before they turn it over to you to take home. Most of the time, everything on the bike will work just right. But some parts may be slightly out of adjustment, so it's best to give your new bike a brief "shake-down cruise" before you leave the shop.

Before you get on the bike, check to see that the changes you specified were made. Next, check to see that the quick-release hubs are adjusted properly and closed tightly. If you're not sure how they work, ask the salesperson. Have him or her show you how to remove a wheel (especially the rear wheel).

Check the brakes. Ask how to use the quick-releases or barrel cable adjusters if you don't know. Squeeze tightly on the levers to make sure the cable ends are fully seated—the last thing you want is for a cable to pop loose when you need to come to a stop.

Finally, take the bike for a short ride. Test both brakes—they should work smoothly and progressively. The brake pads should be far enough from the rims that they don't grab as soon as you apply the brakes, but they should be close enough so you can't pull the levers all the way to the handlebars, either. If the brakes squeal when you apply them, they just need to have the pads "toed in". Let the salesperson know.

Test the shifting system, too. It should function smoothly and cleanly under moderate and hard pedal pres-

Steve Broaddus

(Right) You can climb hills in or out of the saddle, depending on your strength and the length and grade of the hill. Jeff Spencer, 1972 Olympic cyclist, demonstrates proper technique.

John Lehrer

(Left) Take your new bike back after thirty days so that the shop's mechanics can tune it up, adjusting the derailleurs, brakes, and other components.

sure. (Don't shift into a lower gear in the middle of a hill, though. Although contemporary indexed shifting systems can usually handle such shifts, it places an unnecessary strain on them.)

After riding your bike for a week, check it over thoroughly to make sure all cables and bolts are firmly secured. The bike should still ride silently. If a brake pad rubs against the rim, for instance, take it to the shop to have it checked out. Better yet, try to figure out what's wrong yourself. It could be that the brake is out of adjustment or that the wheel is out of true.

Usually, the brake and shifter cables will stretch a little in the first few weeks of use. You may need to take up the slack by tightening the barrel adjusters; indexed shifting systems especially, need to have proper cable tension maintained in order to work correctly.

After the first 250 miles (400 kilometers) of riding, the crank arms may need to be tightened by removing the dust caps and using a ratchet and socket (usually 14 or 15 millimeters) or a crank tool. Don't wait until you hear the crank arms creaking; tighten the bolts as a preventive measure.

Of course, keep your tires properly inflated with a floor pump, and inspect them before each ride to see that the tread or sidewalls haven't become cut from glass or debris.

Finally, pay attention to the steering on your bike. If it feels loose after a few rides, it may be that the headset has become loose. To check this, straddle the bike and firmly apply the front brake. Rock the bike front-to-back; if you feel play or hear a clunking sound, it means the headset is loose. Return the bike to the shop for adjustment.

In any case, take advantage of the thirty-day free tune-up most shops offer with the sale of a new bike. Make an appointment to have your bike serviced even if it seems to be running well. An experienced mechanic may be able to detect a problem that you've missed. For more complete information, check the chapter on maintenance later in this book.

BUYING A USED BIKE

There's another way to buy a quality bike that's especially appealing if you don't have the money to buy a new one. Buying a top-quality, used bike is a fairly safe proposition. Here's why you might consider it:

First, most of the parts on a bicycle are right out in the open where you can see them. Those that aren't, such as the bearings and surfaces in hubs, bottom bracket, and headset, can be inspected fairly easily. In either case, if something works, you (or a more-experienced friend) will be able to tell right away; if it doesn't, you'll know immediately, too.

Second, most owners of bikes costing more than $600 take pretty good care of them. Many people who buy expensive bicycles accumulate several in the course of a few years. Like some sports car owners, some high-quality bike owners get bored with perfectly good bikes when the latest high-tech model hits their bike shop. You can take advantage of this and pick up a great bike for two-thirds or less of what such a bike would cost new.

The best places to find good used bikes are through friends, local cycling publications, and pro bike shops. Many pro shops have bulletin boards listing bikes for sale, and for a reasonable fee, you can probably get the mechanics at the shop to check out any bike you find listed. Also, some shops sell good-quality used bikes on consignment.

Newspapers are generally *not* a good source of quality bikes, but local cycling publications—usually printed monthly—often are. You might also check the newsletters of local cycling clubs for bike listings.

Once you've found a used bike you're interested in buying, there are several things you must determine:

First, of course, be sure that the bike is the right size for you—not only in terms of the frame, but also the major components.

Second, you must make sure that the bike is in good mechanical condition, and if it's not, consider whether it's worth buying and fixing up. You can fix it up in one of two ways: pay a mechanic you trust to check out the bike, or do it yourself (again, preferably with the help of an experienced cycling friend).

If you check the bike out yourself, here's what to look for: First, be sure that the person selling the bike actually owns it. You don't want to become part of a stolen-bike ring. Sometimes you can determine this indirectly, but if in doubt, ask for proof.

Once you've established ownership, look over the bike's frame. Especially check where the tubes are joined. You'll probably see a few scratches on the bike but beware of any dents in the tubing or cracks in the paint, which indicate the bike has been in a crash. (If the paint looks *too* good, find out if the bike has been in an accident, repaired, and repainted.) Be sure to check the fork, as well. Look carefully at the components— brake levers, the undersides of pedal cages, and the rear derailleur—most likely to contact the ground if the bike was in an accident or dropped hard.

Jeffrey E. Blackman

Next to the frame, the wheels are the most important part of the bike—and the most expensive to repair. Spin the wheels to look for irregularities or dents in the rims; take the wheels off the bike and turn the axles to check for proper hub adjustment. Also, check for uniform spoke tension. Make sure the tires are in good shape and are free from cuts or bulges in the sidewalls.

Check the powertrain next. Grab the crank arms and check for play. If you find looseness, it may only mean that the crank arms need to be tightened, but it could mean that the bottom bracket is out of adjustment and may require repair or replacement. Check the chainwheels to see whether they're warped or have any bent teeth.

Examine all components for signs of wear, rust, and corrosion; remove the seat post and look inside the seat tube, too. Note whether the bike has any extras that you'd have to add to the cost of a new bike: toe clips and straps, water bottles and cages, or a pump. Remember, a bike that seems like a bargain at first may not be one when you include the price of repairs or replacement parts, and the labor to install them.

Next take the bike for a test ride. If it's in good shape, it should feel very much like a new bike. Apply the same standards listed earlier for test riding a new bike at a shop.

Finally, keep in mind that buying a used bike is probably only a good idea if you're considering an expensive bike—one that new would sell for $600 and up. This is true for two reasons: First, the quality of the bearings and other components is much better on more expensive bikes; if you buy a used entry-level bike, you're more likely to have to replace worn parts than if you buy a more expensive bike that's been ridden the same amount. Even more important, you won't save much by buying a used bike that costs between $300–$500 when new. If you're considering a bike in this price range, it's probably worth it to spend the extra $75–$100 and get a brand-new bike, with perhaps more advanced technology (such as indexed shifting), a free, thirty-day tune-up, and a new-bike warranty.

Buying a used bicycle can be the way to go if you have lust in your heart but only dust in your wallet.

Bicycle Equipment and Accessories

A s you have no doubt discovered by now, the sport of cycling is an equipment fanatic's delight (or nightmare, depending on the state of your finances). I think it's safe to say that no other athletic endeavor has the variety and sheer number of after-market items, accessories, and related equipment that cycling has; you can easily spend as much on equipment and accessories as you can on your bicycle itself. While few accessories are absolutely essential, most cycling-related products make riding more convenient, enjoyable, and safe.

Bicycle equipment and accessories fall into three categories: those that are added to and become a part of the bicycle itself; those that pertain mostly to the bike, but are separate from it; and those that pertain mostly to the rider.

Equipment that becomes a part of the bicycle includes the following:

Toe clips and straps—Toe clips and straps come as standard equipment on many bicycles costing more than $400. They're essential for a couple of reasons: They keep your feet in the proper position on the pedal (ball of foot over pedal axle) and they allow you to increase your pedaling power by pulling on the upstroke rather than simply pushing down on the pedals. Because they secure your feet to the pedals,

The proper tools, carried under your saddle, will keep you rolling through most on-the-road breakdowns.

they're helpful in hill climbing, when you're standing up to increase your climbing ability. Road riders have used clips and straps for decades; more and more off-road cyclists are beginning to put clips and straps on their mountain bikes.

Toe clips and straps require a few rides to get used to; you have to practice flipping over the pedal with the toe of your foot (by *feel*, not by sight) to get it in the clip, and you have to practice pulling your foot out of the clip when you stop. The best place to practice this is a vacant parking lot.

One of the biggest fears novice cyclists have is that they'll fall over on their bikes because their feet will get trapped in the toe clips if they need to stop suddenly. This rarely happens—or at least there's no reason for it to happen. Just don't pull the toe strap too tight around your foot, especially if you're wearing cleated shoes.

Also, be sure to get the right size of toe clip, which should allow one-eighth to one-quarter inch of room between the toe of your shoe and the clip if you're wearing cleated shoes. In the past year, nylon toe clips and plastic straps, which are lighter and more durable than steel or alloy clips and leather straps, have been introduced. Both clips and straps come in many colors, are made for both quill and platform pedals, and have proved very popular.

Tool kit and frame pump—necessary for roadside repairs (mostly fixing flat tires). This should consist of an under-the-seat pack (made of Cordura nylon, these come in a variety of sizes and colors), a patch kit, spare tube, tire tools, screwdriver, Allen wrenches, spare change, and other

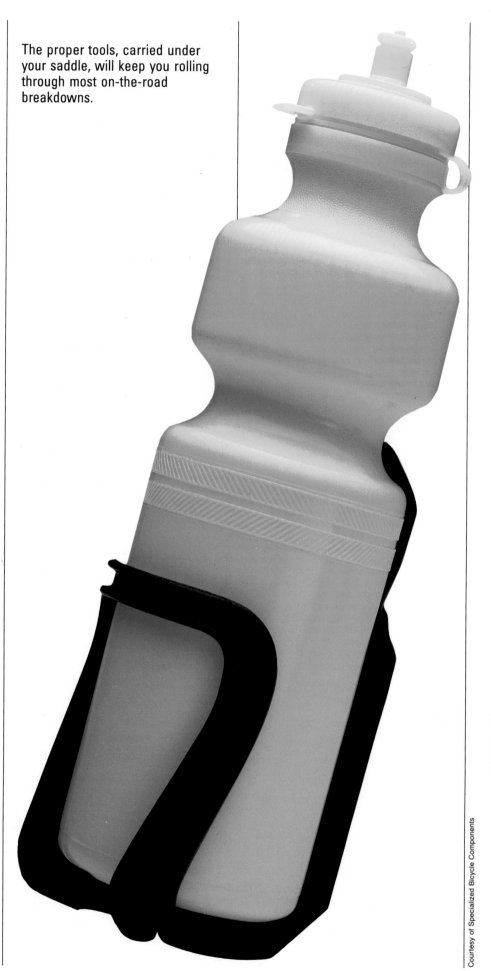

(Left) Large-size bottle and graphite cage, both by Specialized.

Steve Broaddus

odds and ends. (See the maintenance chapter for more information). The frame pump should fit snugly against the front of the seat tube, or under the top tube if you have more than one water bottle. Be sure that the pump head fits the kind of valves you have on your tires (Presta or Schrader).

Water bottle(s) and cage(s)—to keep you from becoming dehydrated, especially on long training rides. Water bottle cages come in any number of colors and materials (generally aluminum alloy; carbon fiber is a recent development). Be sure to get sturdy cages and flexible bottles (they squirt liquid better) with tops that open easily. Among the best cages are those made by Specialized and Blackburn; Specialized makes more water bottles than anyone else; they also make the best ones.

Alternative pedal systems—Along with indexed shifting, this is the biggest development in cycling equipment in this decade. Cleated shoes, along with toe straps and pedals, have been an essential element of efficient cycling for years, because they make the cyclist an integral part of the bicycle's power train. The problem with the system of cleated shoes/toe clips/straps is that in order to ride efficiently, the cyclist has to strap his feet tightly into the toe clips, reducing circulation and producing numb feet, and creating the possibility of getting trapped in the toe clips in an emergency. Also a cyclist can still feel "slop" in his or her feet when climbing a hill or sprinting hard.

Clipless/strapless systems (as we'll refer to them generically) have changed all that. There are presently about a half-dozen such systems on the market, ranging in price from about $50 to $125. (All, but one, Cycle Binding, require the cyclist to wear cleated shoes.) Many of these systems are adapted from ski-binding applications. Typically, there is a wedge-shaped cleat attached to the bottom of the cyclist's shoe that slips into a slot or cage attached to a pedal axle. Part of the cage is spring-loaded, so that the cleat snaps in and remains secure

Gary Marcus/Shimano America

Clipless/strapless pedal systems, such as these by Shimano, (about $140), are an extremely popular cycling accessory.

when the cyclist pulls his or her foot up, pushes it down or moves it backward or forward. As with ski bindings, a sideways twist releases the foot immediately.

These systems, which became popular in 1986, are past the testing stage of development. The bugs have been eliminated, the systems work, and they're here to stay. Bike shops that serve serious recreational cyclists, as well as triathletes and racers, accumulate boxes of conventional pedals while strapless/clipless systems sell out. While these pedal systems are far from essential and have yet to appear as standard equipment on a production bike (some say it's just a matter of time), virtually everyone who tries them likes them. Cyclists are installing them on bikes costing as little as $400 or as much as $2000; mountain bike riders are even starting to bolt them to cyclocross shoes.

By far the most popular of these binding systems is the Look System imported by Descente. The company also makes its own shoes that are specially drilled and constructed for its cleats. (You can use conventional cleated shoes with Look pedals and with some of the other systems; indeed, many are drilled out to take the Look cleat. But you often have to install a homemade nylon strap around any shoe not specifically designed for strapless/clipless pedal systems. Otherwise, the uppers of these shoes sometimes separate from the soles.)

Computers—This is another accessory that's hardly essential but still highly popular, and for good reason. Who wouldn't be willing to spend $30–$40 on a little black box that weighs about two ounces, is about the size of an audio cassette, and reliably tells a rider (at the very least) the current speed, trip distance, total distance, and elapsed time? (Some computers feature average speed, cadence, maximum speed, time of day, multiple alarms, and so on.) Bicycle computers are useful as motivators to improve your cycling—they're popular with athletes, who use them (sometimes along with heart-rate monitors) as training aids, as well as with recreational cyclists, who just want to know the distance of their weekend rides. There are about a dozen currently available; they've been around since 1984, are generally easy to mount and use, and are reliable and durable. Dependable brands include Cat-Eye and Avocet.

Tires and tubes—Tires and tubes fall under the category of replacement parts, but because they're replaced so frequently, it makes sense to consider recent developments here. In the past two or three years, the cycling industry has made tremendous strides producing durable, high-performance, wired-on ("clincher") tires. Compared to the tires that were on the market as recently as five years ago, today's bicycle tires are lighter, more responsive, and more resistant to punctures than ever before. There are also a greater variety of tread patterns (for both road and off-road use) to accommodate varied terrain and road-surface conditions better. The top-quality tires now available have a high thread count in the sidewall (making them more resilient); and many have a belt of Kevlar under the contact surface (making them highly puncture-resistant).

Mountain bike tires come in dozens of variations for a wide range of off-road cycling applications.

John Lehrer

(Top) Electronic cycling computers keep track of current speed, time, trip and total distances, and more.
(Bottom) Spenco grips use a nylon-covered gel material to provide superior cushioning.

In the past two years, polyurethane inner tubes have been invented, and while they're not yet as popular as conventional rubber tubes, they seem to work well. They're a little less flexible than rubber tubes, but a bit lighter and far more resistant to punctures. (They also require their own patch kits; conventional glue and patches won't adhere to polyurethane tubes.)

Grips/handlebar tape—Bicycles generally come equipped with thin, colored plastic handlebar tape, which has been the standard of racers and recreational cyclists alike for years. A proven alternative for those who prefer a bit more padding but want to maintain a strong sense of handlebar control is Spenco grips, a thin, nylon-covered, gel-like material that both looks good and does a fine job of cushioning the handlebars. Also available is a thicker, padded plastic handlebar tape.

The second category of bicycle accessories and equipment, bike-related products that are separate

Spenco

For night-time and off-season training, it's hard to beat the benefits of a wind trainer. Shown: Slocum Prime and Blackburn RX-2.

from the bicycle itself, includes the following:

Floor pump—Because they continuously lose air pressure, bicycle tires need to be pumped up before each ride. Hand (frame-fit) pumps aren't intended to be used to inflate tires to over 100 pounds of pressure on a daily basis. Using the air hose at your local gas station is a bad idea, too—it releases a large volume of air at high pressure that can easily blow a tire off a rim. It's also very difficult to modulate service station hoses.

A floor pump makes it simple, easy, and safe to maintain proper air pressure in your tires. The best ones are made by Silca and Zefal; they cost $30–$40 and last a lifetime with minimal maintenance.

Wind trainer—This is the generic name for a clever training device that was invented about 1980; it's a stand you clamp your bike to (usually by the front fork), with a roller under the rear wheel that has small cylinders with fan blades attached. You ride your bike in place—no balancing skill is required—and the cylinders turn, catching the air and providing resistance.

Wind trainers are invaluable training devices for riders who want to maintain cycling fitness in inclement weather, or for those who can only find time to train when the sun has gone down. They're far more sensible than an exercise bicycle because they let you ride your own bike, which fits you better than an exercise bike ever could. The latest versions of these machines feature weighted (and sometimes magnetized) flywheels in addition to turbo fans, which help eliminate the noise created by fans. Some of the better trainers are made by Slocum, Minoura, Blackburn, and Vetta.

Bicycle racks—More and more

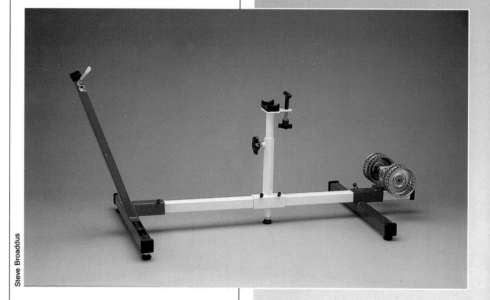

Steve Broaddus

dedicated cyclists welcome the opportunity to take their bicycles with them when they take an automobile trip. That's easy and safe to do since the development of car-mounted racks that carry up to six bicycles. There are two basic types: trunk-mounted racks and roof-mounted racks.

Trunk-mounted racks are inexpensive, easy to attach and remove from your car, and can accommodate two or three bikes in safety. When using trunk racks, it's important to put padding between the bikes to keep them from scratching each other and your car. The best thing to use is called Protect-o-Pads, made by Graber Products Corporation. They are dense foam blocks that attach to your bike's frame, and are available at your bike shop. The disadvantages of trunk racks are that they don't attach to the car as solidly as do roof racks, and you can't attach your bicycle as securely to a trunk rack as you can to a roof rack. Trunk racks are more likely to damage a car's finish, and it's easier for bikes on trunk racks to bump into each other, marring the bike's paint

Blackburn

John Lehrer

This ultralight Giro helmet and Oakley Blades (left) and cycling hat and Oakley Factory Pilots (right) are the latest in fashionable, high-tech protection.

job as well. Also, bikes on trunk racks are more susceptible to damage in rear-end accidents and from the automobile's exhaust. Trunk racks best suit the needs of cyclists who only want to transport their bikes by car infrequently and for short distances. The best trunk racks are made by Rhode Gear, Hollywood Engineering, and Graber Products.

Roof racks, on the other hand, are versatile devices that mount easily on your car roof, usually by clamping on the rain gutters, and that can generally be adapted to carry a variety of sporting equipment (surfboards, skis, canoes, kayaks) and other gear. Roof racks, once they're adjusted, take only five to ten minutes to install or remove, but many cyclists leave them on their cars all the time. Roof racks

attach securely to your car, and it's easy to attach your bikes (up to six) tightly to them, usually by clamping the front fork dropouts in a quick-release skewer on the rack that's just like the one on a front bike wheel.

Roof racks are expensive, but they're durable, versatile, and reliable, and the only solution for cyclists who want to transport their bikes by car frequently—after all, you can't just stuff a high-quality bike into your trunk. The best roof racks are made by Yakima and Thule.

Lights—A lighting system is essential for cyclists who must ride after dark. In the past, several primitive devices were available: battery-operated lights that a rider strapped to his or her leg, which allowed cars to be aware of the cyclist but were useless

for lighting the road, and generator-powered headlights and taillights that required continuous adjustment and maintenance. Contemporary lighting systems are compact and easy to use, and feature high-intensity, quartz-halogen bulbs and rechargeable gel-cell or ni-cad batteries.

Locks—Cyclists are justifiably concerned about the possibility that their beautiful bicycles may be ripped off—hundreds of thousands are stolen every year, and very few are recovered. There are four levels of security available; pick the one that best fits your circumstances. The very least you can do is always keep your eye on your bike whenever you park it, or be sure that it's in a locked room. Second, you can buy an inexpensive, thin wire cable with a lock attached. These are easy to store in an under-the-seat bag and will keep the casual thief from riding off with your bike while you're picking up a soda in the local 7-Eleven. However, wire cutters can slice through such a cable.

There are heavier cables and locks

that are easy to carry in a jersey pocket. They're the kind you'd use if you were taking a ride with a group of cyclists and wanted to stop for breakfast. You can lock up your bike outside the restaurant and not have to keep an eye on it all the time; such cables can only be sheared by heavy-duty bolt cutters.

Finally, there are U-shaped locks such as those made by Citadel and Kryptonite. They're a bit cumbersome to carry, but they're an excellent choice for commuters or any cyclist who parks in the same place all the time; the lock can often be left where you keep your bike. These locks are impervious to practically any attempt to destroy them.

The third and final category is cycling accessories and equipment that pertain mostly to the rider—in other words, cycling clothing. Many riders buy and wear cycling apparel because it's fashionable—because they want the "look." That's fine, but, like most other athletic wear, cycling clothing is functional, too. In the last few years, cycling wear has become very colorful, a welcome departure from the days when it was dowdy and dreadfully dull.

Taking it from the top:

Helmets—The most valuable item of cycling clothing you can wear is a helmet. Every year, thousands of cyclists are involved in accidents that require hospitalization; about 1000 die, 75 percent of them from head injuries. In many of these accidents, the cyclist's life could have been saved if he or she had been wearing an appropriate cycling helmet. Helmets have received a boost since the United States Cycling Federation made hard-shell helmets mandatory for USCF-sponsored races, beginning in 1986. The USCF dragged its feet for years on the matter, mainly because American racers, imitating the "macho" attitude of European riders, opposed the use of hard-shell helmets, wearing instead leather "hairnets," which provided minimal protection.

Thankfully, hairnets are gone—what you should look for is a helmet that passes the American National Standards Institute (ANSI) Z90.4 drop test. It usually will have a hard outer shell and an expanded polystyrene bead (Styrofoam) liner. In case you're in an accident involving a blow to your head, the liner deforms, destroying itself but absorbing the force that would otherwise be transmitted to your brain. Lest you think helmets are only for speed merchants and racers, consider this: Standing still, if you were to fall and strike your head on the pavement, the force could be sufficient to cause a fatal injury.

A dozen or more brands of helmets are available in a variety of shapes, sizes, and colors. (The lightest ANSI-approved helmet currently available, the Giro Sport, which protects with Styrofoam, has no hard outer shell and weighs about eight ounces.) Find a helmet that passes the ANSI Z90.4 test, offers sufficient ventilation, and fits your head comfortably. That's all you need to know to keep your head in one piece.

Hats—Hats serve a different purpose than helmets; worn under a helmet, traditional cycling caps are useful to keep perspiration from running into your eyes. Winter hats feature ear flaps to keep you warm.

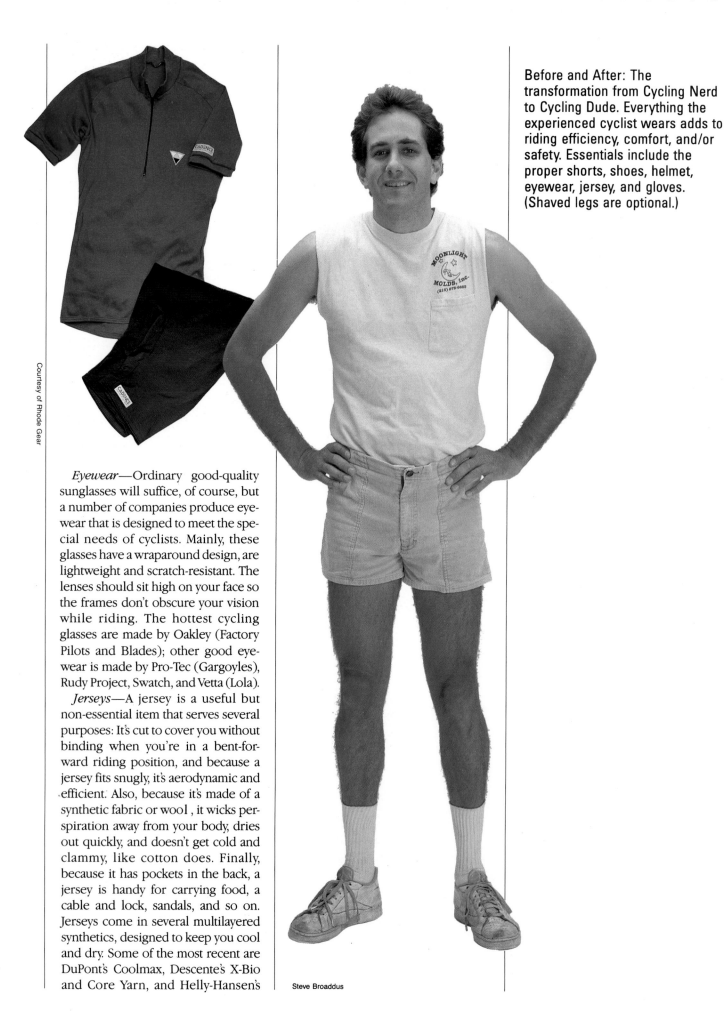

Courtesy of Rhode Gear

Steve Broaddus

Before and After: The transformation from Cycling Nerd to Cycling Dude. Everything the experienced cyclist wears adds to riding efficiency, comfort, and/or safety. Essentials include the proper shorts, shoes, helmet, eyewear, jersey, and gloves. (Shaved legs are optional.)

Eyewear—Ordinary good-quality sunglasses will suffice, of course, but a number of companies produce eyewear that is designed to meet the special needs of cyclists. Mainly, these glasses have a wraparound design, are lightweight and scratch-resistant. The lenses should sit high on your face so the frames don't obscure your vision while riding. The hottest cycling glasses are made by Oakley (Factory Pilots and Blades); other good eyewear is made by Pro-Tec (Gargoyles), Rudy Project, Swatch, and Vetta (Lola).

Jerseys—A jersey is a useful but non-essential item that serves several purposes: It's cut to cover you without binding when you're in a bent-forward riding position, and because a jersey fits snugly, it's aerodynamic and efficient. Also, because it's made of a synthetic fabric or wool, it wicks perspiration away from your body, dries out quickly, and doesn't get cold and clammy, like cotton does. Finally, because it has pockets in the back, a jersey is handy for carrying food, a cable and lock, sandals, and so on. Jerseys come in several multilayered synthetics, designed to keep you cool and dry. Some of the most recent are DuPont's Coolmax, Descente's X-Bio and Core Yarn, and Helly-Hansen's

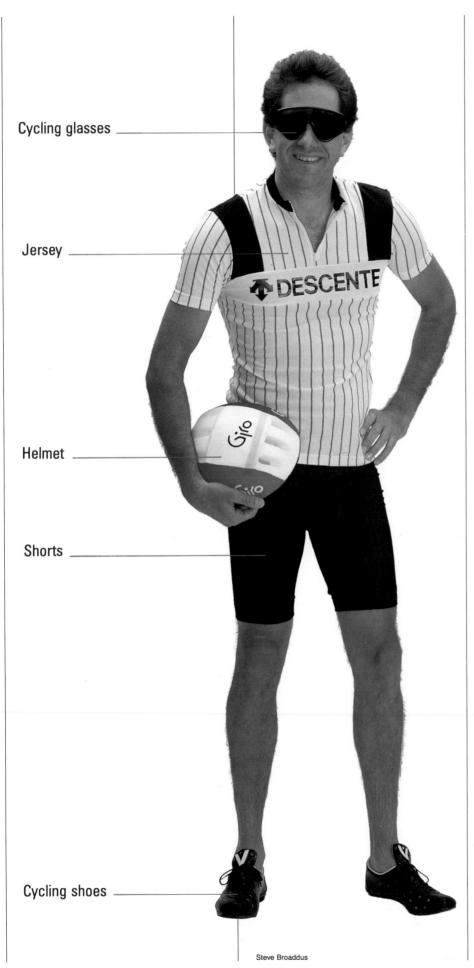

Cycling glasses

Jersey

DESCENTE

Helmet

Shorts

Cycling shoes

Steve Broaddus

Steve Broaddus

Steve Broaddus

Helly-Tech and Sport-Tech.

Cycling shorts—Next to your helmet, cycling shorts are the most important item of cycling apparel in your wardrobe. They're critical to your comfort on medium- and long-distance rides. First and foremost, they have no seams anywhere that your rear end meets the seat, which effectively prevents blisters and saddle sores. Second, they have a chamois crotch (genuine leather or a synthetic) to absorb perspiration and provide padding. Finally, they extend to mid-thigh to prevent your legs from chafing against the saddle. Most riders consider form-fitting "racing" shorts superior to looser "touring" shorts, which often bunch up and chafe. Touring shorts, with pockets and a looser fit, may appeal to the less hard-core rider.

Gloves—Cycling gloves are important for several reasons: They keep your hands from becoming painful or numb on long rides; they protect your hands in case of an accident; and they're useful to wipe glass and other sharp objects from your tires. Recent styles come with mesh, Lycra, or terrycloth backs. Be sure to choose a pair that gives both sufficient cushion and handlebar "feel."

Steve Broaddus

Cycling shoes—a very functional piece of cycling wear. You'll notice right away the difference cycling shoes can make, especially on any ride more than twenty miles. Cycling shoes come in three varieties: cleated, touring, and mountain bike shoes. Cleated shoes are strictly for road use, touring shoes can be used for road or trail riding, and mountain bike shoes are best suited for off-road use. The principal difference between cycling shoes and other athletic shoes is that cycling shoes have rigid, unyielding soles, which serves two purposes: By minimizing unnecessary flex, it prevents the waste of energy by more effectively transmitting the rider's effort through the pedals to the bicycle's drivetrain. The stiff sole also minimizes the amount of pedal pressure that gets through to the rider's foot, increasing foot comfort.

Cleated cycling shoes are most efficient, especially when combined with one of the clipless/strapless pedal systems. The only real problem is that they're uncomfortable to walk in; riders who wear cleated cycling shoes often carry a pair of sandals in their jersey to walk in if they're going to spend much time off the bike. Touring shoes are probably best for all-around use; they're not as stiff and efficient as cleated shoes, but they're a big improvement over running-type shoes for riding, and as comfortable as any shoes to walk in. Mountain bike shoes need to be versatile, so they're similar to touring shoes, but they're more ruggedly built (and a bit heavier). Their soles are often wider, too, making it difficult to use them on road bike pedals.

Foul-weather clothing—This category takes into account any clothing needed to keep you warm and dry in inclement weather—wind suits, tights, rain suits, arm and leg warmers, full-fingered gloves, and waterproof caps. This stuff is all lightweight and pretty high-tech. Don't look just for coated nylon taffeta or ripstop nylon anymore. Look instead for DuPont Thermax and Supplex, Gore-Tex, Burlington's Versatech, and Maiden Mills' Polarplus 6. These fabrics are supplanting polypropylene, which wicks away moisture but absorbs (and retains) body odors. Most bike shops advise that if you want wool clothing, buy it now. It, too, is quickly being replaced by high-tech synthetics.

With this variety of gear, all it takes is a little dedication to keep on cycling in almost any kind of weather.

It's tempting to say that the biggest developments in cycling equipment and accessories have already occurred, but that would be foolish. Still, there are very few needs that haven't already been well-met; in every area, equipment is far more refined today than it was just five years ago—more durable, better-finished, lighter, more "user-friendly." The upper limits of refinement haven't been reached, but it's also safe to say that very few cycling products and accessories being produced today will be outmoded or obsolete five years from now.

Courtesy of Specialized Bicycle Components

Mountain bike shoes (left) and the latest for the road warrior (below). Cold-weather riding requires gloves, long sleeves, tights, and windproof fabrics (right)

Jeffrey E. Blackman

Basic Elements of Bike Fit

So far, the focus of this book has been on how to buy equipment—now the focus changes to how to *use* your new bicycle and equipment.

In Chapter Three, you learned how to determine the correct frame size for your bicycle, but that's only part of the story. The next step has two parts: first, to adjust the various components of your bike to custom-fit it to your body dimensions and type of riding; and second, to adjust your body posture while riding for optimum comfort and efficiency.

When you first purchase your new bike, many shops will give you a preliminary fitting to adjust the bike's dimensions to your body size and riding style. Some may even have a sophisticated fitting system such as the Fit-Kit,® which provides excellent general guidelines. But your final adjustments can only be determined by a gradual process of experimentation, and some will change over the course of time as you become a more experienced and proficient rider.

The fact is, if your bike isn't adjusted to fit you, you won't enjoy riding it nearly as much. You also risk injury—damage to joints, muscles, or connective tissue—by riding a bike that doesn't fit correctly. So first, here's a systematic, step-by-step analysis that will help you understand the intricacies of the bike-body relationship so that you can make the proper adjustments to your own bike.

If possible, have an experienced cyclist assist you with the adjustments you make to your bike—it's helpful to get feedback from someone who can observe things about your riding position that you're unable to detect while on the bike. The safest and simplest way to adjust your bike is to set it up on a wind trainer. If you don't own or can't borrow one, a friend can hold your bike in an upright position while you simulate riding positions on it. Be sure to wear the shorts and shoes you'd normally wear while riding.

You'll be making adjustments to your bike at the three points your body makes contact with it—the seat, the pedals, and the handlebars. Make the changes in this order:

Foot position—The ball of your foot should be over the pedal axle. If it's not, you'll waste energy and put undue stress on your knees. Achieving this position depends on choosing the appropriate length of toe clip. If you ride in cleated shoes, choose a toe clip that allows one-eighth to one-quarter inch (about two-thirds centimeter) between the toe of your shoe and the clip. (Also, be sure your cleats are correctly aligned.) If you wear street shoes or touring shoes, it's okay for the toe of your shoe to touch the front of the clip. It's better to have clips that are slightly too long than too short. If your foot falls between sizes (S, M, L, X-L), use washers to shim the clips, go to the next largest size, or check out another brand (Japanese clips are smaller than European makes).

Saddle height—Correct seat height is crucial to your cycling efficiency and enjoyment. If you set the seat too high, you'll rock back and forth on the saddle as you pedal, which becomes very painful in your rear end and crotch after a few miles. On the other hand, if you set the saddle too low, you won't get maximum force from the pedal stroke, and the muscles in the front of your thighs (quadriceps) will become sore after a long ride.

Here's how to determine correct saddle height. Remove the toe clips from the pedals, and with the bike secured to the trainer (or held steadily by your friend while you sit on it),

get on the seat and place the heels of your shoes on the pedal axles. Pedal backward slowly, and pay attention to your leg position when either pedal is at the bottom of the stroke. If the saddle height is correct, your leg will be fully extended, but your pelvis will remain stationary on the saddle while you pedal. It's easy enough to check your own leg extension, but you'll need someone to stand behind you to watch your hips to check for pelvic movement while you pedal. If your pelvis rocks back and forth while you pedal, lower the seat; if your leg is bent, raise the seat.

The longer you've been riding with your seat in a particular position, the smaller your adjustments to saddle height should be, because you'll need to give your tendons and muscles a chance to adjust themselves gradually to the new position. If you've been riding for years with your saddle an inch higher than you now think it should be, lower it a fraction of an inch several times over the period of a month. If you're just getting back into

riding after a long layoff, lower the saddle all at once and get used to it.

Next, put the toe clips back on, sit in the saddle and pedal normally. Your pelvis should not rock and there should be a slight bend in your knee at the bottom of the stroke. Two other things should be taken into account when you set the saddle height: foot size and foot movement while pedaling. If you have large feet and point your toes down while pedaling, you'll need to set your seat higher than a rider with small feet who pedals flat-footed.

Other saddle adjustments—Your saddle also needs to be adjusted properly front-to-back and given the correct tilt. Some authorities dispute the importance of the front-to-back saddle adjustment, but most still agree that as a general rule, you should position the saddle front-to-back on the seat post so that when the crank arms of your bike are horizontal, your forward knee joint is centered over the pedal axle.

To make this adjustment, loosen the saddle clamp slightly and sit on

(Left) For best foot position, the ball of your foot should be over the pedal axle. With cleated shoes, there should be one-eighth to one-quarter inch of space between the end of your toe and the toe clip.

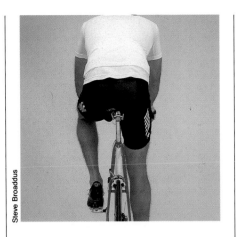

Steve Broaddus

(Below) If your saddle is the proper height, when your heel is placed over the pedal axle, your leg should be completely extended. (Left) Viewed from behind, your pelvis should not rock when you pedal.

Steve Broaddus

(Right) Most riders find a level saddle most comfortable. (Below) A plumb bob, extended from the tibial tuberosity when your foot is in the 3 o'clock position, should pass through or just behind the pedal axle. This indicates proper front-to-back seat position.

Steve Broaddus

(Right) To achieve proper handlebar tilt and brake lever position, start with the top of the bars level or tilted slightly downward. Brake levers should be placed where your hands can reach them easily from the top of the bars.

Steve Broaddus

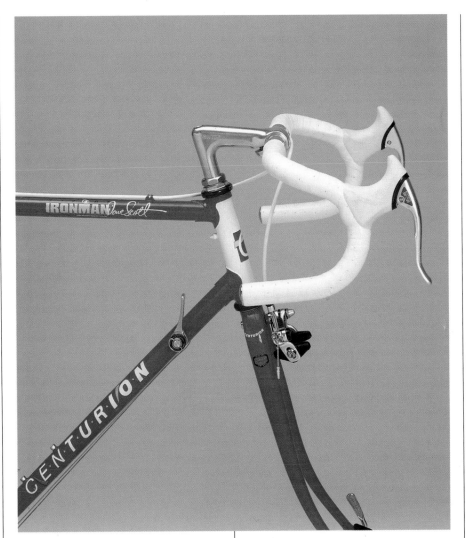

the saddle at the point most comfortable for you. With your feet in the toe clips, move the crank arms so they're horizontal (with the pedals at the three and nine o'clock positions). Hold a plumb bob (or a string weighted with an Allen wrench) against the bony bump (the tibial tuberosity) on your shinbone about two inches below your kneecap. If your saddle is in the correct fore-aft position, the weighted string will bisect the pedal axle, or fall up to three-quarters of an inch behind it. If the string falls in front of the pedal axle, move your seat back; if the string falls behind the rear of the pedal cage, move your seat forward. When you've got the saddle in the correct position, tighten the clamp on the seat post. Remember that moving the seat forward puts you closer to the pedals. If you make a big fore-aft seat adjustment, you'll have to readjust the saddle height to compensate.

Finally, adjust the tilt of the saddle.

For most people, a level saddle or one whose nose tilts upward slightly works best. Some riders with sore crotches or rear ends try to solve that problem by tilting the nose of their saddle downward. The difficulty with that "solution" is that when the nose of the saddle tilts down, you constantly slide forward, putting too much of your weight on the handlebars. Keeping the saddle level or tipped up slightly will ensure that the fore-aft position of your pelvis will remain stable, giving you a better sense of balance and more control on your bike.

Handlebar adjustments—The adjustments you've made so far affect primarily the relationship of your lower body to your bike; the correct guidelines for determining seat position vary little from rider to rider, regardless of ability or preferred riding style.

It's a different story with adjustments to your handlebars, which

affect your upper-body position. The optimum handlebar position, which determines whether you sit relatively upright or bent over on your bike, can vary considerably and will depend on your reasons for cycling and the length of time you've been riding. Older riders, tourists, and novices, for example, usually prefer to sit more upright (handlebars higher and farther back) than cyclists who ride competitively. Riders who want to go fast will choose a more aerodynamic, horizontal torso position. The guidelines stated here are intended as a starting point for casual, touring, or sport riders, who benefit from a slightly more upright posture than racers use.

If your frame size (including the top tube length) generally is correct for your body type, you can make adjustments to how upright or bent-over you ride by the length of stem you install on your bike. Stems are non-adjustable, so if your stem is the wrong length, you'll have to replace it. (Most dealers will exchange the stock stem on a new bike if it's the wrong size.) It's more important to replace your stem if it's too long, because being too stretched out on your bike causes a variety of uncomfortable situations—a sore crotch, sore neck and shoulders, and sore wrists.

To tell whether your stem size is correct, sit on the saddle, reach forward, and grasp the bars just above the brake levers, making sure that you bend at the waist and keep your back straight. Have your partner check the angle of your torso—it should be about forty-five degrees. If it's lower than that, or if your upper arm and torso form an angle greater than ninety degrees, you need a shorter stem. This method is based on the length of your arms and torso together, which makes it more useful than others based on torso length alone.

Next, you're ready to set stem height, which refers to how much of your handlebar stem extends vertically from your bike's head tube. Most stems have a minimum-insertion mark, which indicates the maximum amount that you can safely raise the stem above the top ring of the bike's headset. Set your stem initially according to your body size and

Mountain biking can be a demanding, acrobatic sport calling for agility and upper-body strength. Be sure to position yourself properly on the bike and wear plenty of protective clothing.

Steve Broaddus

riding style; in general, the taller you are and the faster you like to ride, the lower you should set your stem. You can lower the stem, if you like, until your thighs touch—but don't crash into—your rib cage while you pedal.

As is the case with most other bicycle components, handlebars are proportionately sized on modern production bicycles. The most important handlebar dimension is width. Handlebars come in three popular widths—38, 40, and 42 centimeters. The width of the bars should correspond roughly to your shoulder width. Racing cyclists, tall cyclists, and riders with large hands may want bars with more drop (the vertical distance, viewed from the side, from the top to the drops of the bars).

Finally, the tilt of the bars and positioning of the brake levers on the bars is more a matter of comfort than anything else. As a starting point, set the tilt of your bars so that the bottom of the bars is nearly level with the ground or pointed slightly downward; position the brake levers so that their ends are nearly even with the bottom of the bars.

CRITERIA FOR MOUNTAIN BIKE ADJUSTMENTS

The above guidelines apply to road bikes; criteria for off-road riding are somewhat different. Seat-height considerations are the same; the principal difference is the reach to the bars, which is considerably shorter on a mountain bike. Mountain bikes have upright handlebars, which distribute more of the rider's weight onto the saddle. An upright position

(about midway between sitting straight up and the 45-degree bend of a road rider's torso) is more appropriate for a mountain bike because it's more comfortable for riding short distances. (A mountain bike rider receives more pounding up through the handlbars; shifting his or her weight rearward reduces the impact.) Furthermore, an upright seating position lets the mountain bike rider "unload" (take weight off) the front wheel, which is crucial to maintaining control in a hard, fast downhill. It also contributes to better uphill traction, gives a seated rider the leverage to climb a hill while pushing a larger gear than usual, and lets a rider stand up more easily, shifting body weight to maintain traction and stability.

For longer-distance rides or for slogging into the wind on a mountain bike, you can bend forward, forearms horizontal, to simulate the torso position of a road rider.

Unfortunately, stems for mountain bikes aren't yet available in as many lengths as those for road bikes; however, there's a good selection of different handlebars available for mountain bikes, and any bar except one that's completely straight can be rotated in the stem to position the rider's hands (and, therefore, body) differently.

Now that you've custom-tailored your bicycle to your body's dimensions, it's time to make some *adjustments to your riding technique* that will both make you more comfortable on your bike, and a better rider, too. Proper adjustment of your bike doesn't guarantee cycling comfort and efficiency—it only makes them possible. It's not how far you ride, it's how *well* you ride that determines how you feel when you get home.

John Lehrer

ARM, SHOULDER, AND NECK PAIN

Riding comfort depends on proper distribution and support of body weight; ultimately, that's what adjusting your bicycle and riding technique accomplishes. Most beginning cyclists hunch their upper body forward, arching their back, keeping their pelvis upright, lifting their head, straightening their arms and locking their elbows, and putting a considerable amount of upper-body weight on their hands. This forces the wrong muscles—the small muscles in the arms, neck, and shoulder—to do the work of supporting the weight of the upper body. In short order, these riders become tense and constricted; by the end of a long ride, they're invariably sore.

Attention to a few important details can make all the difference in the world as far as riding comfort is concerned. The experienced rider lets his or her legs work hard at propelling the bike forward, allowing the larger, stronger muscles of the lower back and abdomen to support the upper body. Proficient cyclists keep their back straight, tip their pelvis forward, relax their shoulders, and bend their elbows slightly. They move their hands to a variety of handlebar positions in order to distribute body weight among as many muscles as possible.

Begin by trying to become aware of the muscles you use most while cycling. While pedaling on a trainer (or while a friend supports your bicycle), take your hands off the bars and bend forward from the waist until you feel

Steve Broaddus

The differences between the novice rider (left) and the veteran cyclist (right) are tremendous. The novice keeps his pelvis upright, back arched, shoulders hunched, head erect, and arms rigid. By contrast, the experienced rider tilts his pelvis, bends from the waist and keeps his back straight, relaxes his arms and shoulders, and tilts his head forward, rolling his eyes upward to see down the road.

yourself begin to lose your balance. If you can't get down very far until you feel your torso toppling forward, you know that you're putting too much weight on your hands when you ride. (In fact, it's a good training exercise to ride a wind trainer in the bent-over, "no hands" position described above.)

Neck pain is also common among novice cyclists, especially after a ride of several hours. It results primarily from the natural tendency to keep your head erect, which causes no problems when your torso is also ver-

tical. If your upper body is tilted forward at a forty-five degree angle, however, trying to keep your head erect puts an enormous strain on the small, delicate muscles of the neck. Instead of lifting your head continuously, it's better to develop the habit of keeping your neck straight and your head down, and rolling your eyes upward to see what's in the roadway in front of you. When you ride down on the drops, raise your head and torso upward every few pedal strokes so that you can see far enough down the road to avoid danger.

Steve Broaddus

(Above) Pedaling on a trainer with your hands on your thighs will demonstrate if you're putting too much weight on your hands.

Steve Broaddus

Jeffrey E. Blackman

SEAT PAIN

Has there ever lived a cycling enthusiast who hasn't at some time suffered from saddle sores or a rear end that ached? Probably not. Certainly, simple conditioning is a major factor in being able to ride long distances without experiencing rear-end pain; you need to give your body the chance to develop callouses and get accustomed to the shape of your bicycle saddle. If, after several weeks of riding, the situation doesn't seem to be improving, you may need to consider buying a new saddle.

Should you decide that you need a new saddle, go back to the shop where you bought your bike; there's a good chance they'll let you test-ride a few saddles to find one that fits your anatomy better. If you return with your original saddle in new condition a few days after buying your bike, the shop may allow you to exchange the saddle.

Saddle pain occurs because your weight is concentrated on small, sensitive areas of your anatomy. A saddle must be shaped and padded so that it supports both your ischial tuberosities ("sit bones") and genital area; you need proper support on both the front and rear of the saddle.

Steve Broaddus

Steve Broaddus

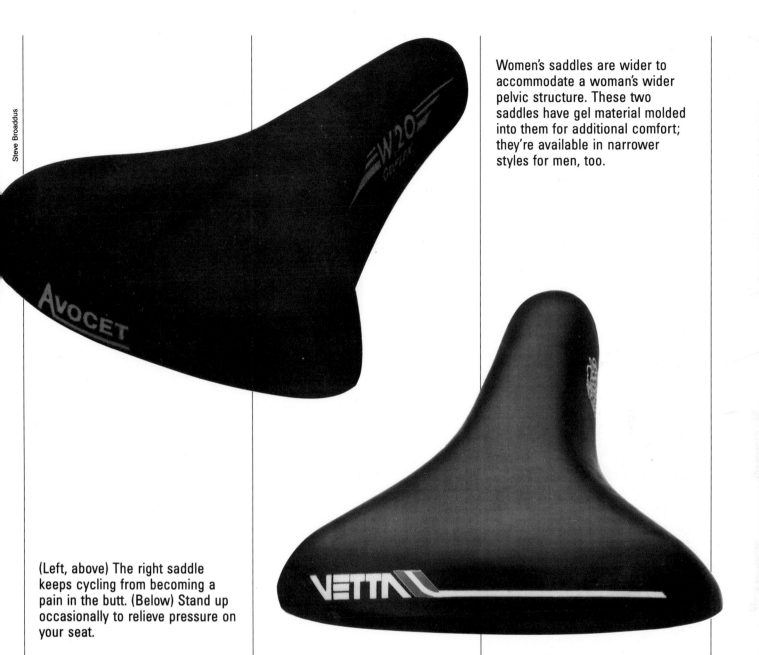

Women's saddles are wider to accommodate a woman's wider pelvic structure. These two saddles have gel material molded into them for additional comfort; they're available in narrower styles for men, too.

(Left, above) The right saddle keeps cycling from becoming a pain in the butt. (Below) Stand up occasionally to relieve pressure on your seat.

The primary factors that determine whether a saddle is comfortable are the shape and flexibility of the shell, and the thickness, density, and location of the padding. A saddle should be as wide as possible for optimum support, but not so wide that your thighs chafe against any part of it. Estimate how wide a saddle you'll need based on the width of your hips; try a wider one first, and go with a slightly narrower one if you feel your thighs rubbing against it. Match the padding on a saddle to the "padding" on your body; the more firm and fit you are, the more weight you'll put on your feet while riding, and the more likely you'll prefer a saddle with minimal padding. If you're a tourist or a mountain bike rider who sits in a more

upright position, you'll probably prefer a saddle with an ample amount of padding in the ischial area.

Female riders have special problems where saddle comfort is concerned. Their ischial bones are almost always more widely spaced than those of men, so they invariably prefer saddles that are wider in the rear. In addition, women often find that they need saddles with noses that are wider and more padded than those that fit men, in order to reduce painful pressure in the genital area.

Noteworthy advances have been made in saddle design in the past few years. Not only are there a great variety of saddle shapes available for both men and women, but saddles are now padded with several different elas-

topolymer gels (under a variety of brand names) that seem to provide better cushion and support. If you have continuing discomfort, it usually means you need a wider saddle, or one with a different shape.

It sometimes helps to relieve rear-end pain to stand up occasionally and pedal for a few minutes at a time. This promotes circulation and cooling, and pedaling while standing gives some leg muscles a rest while working others harder. Another tip is to move around on the saddle to change the points of greatest pressure on your rear. Be sure to lift your rear end off the seat when you go over bumpy sections of road or when you cross railroad tracks. It's easier on your wheels as well as your rear end.

Steve Broaddus

HANDS AND WRISTS

One of the best ways to deal with hand pain, of course, is a good pair of cycling gloves, but it's also a good idea to learn not to support your torso with your arms. In other words, reach out and grasp the bars; don't lean on them. Keep your elbows bent slightly, your wrists straight and relaxed, and change your hand position frequently, moving from the top of the bars, along the bends and out to the brake hoods. A thin, cushioned handlebar cover, such as Spenco grips, also reduces pain and numbness.

Wearing cycling gloves and relaxing your elbows and wrists will help make long rides more comfortable.

The rigid soles of both touring and racing shoes are both more efficient and comfortable.

FEET

Wearing proper cycling shoes contributes tremendously to foot comfort, as well as making you a more efficient cyclist. Cleated shoes, with thicker, more rigid soles, are best for long rides. If the soles of your feet become especially tender, try inserting a Spenco or other padded insole into your shoes. One of the advantages of the new, strapless/clipless pedal systems is that they don't constrict your foot, and therefore promote better circulation, reducing the chance that your feet will become numb on strenuous rides. They also allow you to pull up on the cranks more easily instead of using all your force pushing down on the pedals; this reduces the pressure on the soles of your feet.

The key to adjusting your bicycle and your riding technique is not only to be willing to experiment, but also to make your changes gradually and in small increments. Be methodical—if you only vary one thing at a time, it's much easier to tell why you do or don't like the results. Drastic changes are likely to make you less—not more—comfortable.

As you become a more experienced cyclist, you should find yourself becoming more relaxed on your bike, which may be the most difficult skill of all to master. Remember that developing a comfortable cycling style takes time. If you apply the methods listed here, however, you should feel the results fairly rapidly, and you'll be on the road to greater cycling enjoyment.

Steve Broaddus

Getting the Most from Your Bike

"**O**nce you learn how to ride a bike, you never forget" is the most frequent "old sayings" associated with bicycles. The implication is that anyone can learn to ride a bike—it's child's play, it's easy.

Well, yes—and no. It's one thing to be a youngster riding a bike on the sidewalk, around the block, under the supervision of your parents, and it's another to ride a bike as an adult. As an adult cyclist, you'll be riding your bike in far more demanding circumstances than you did when you were a child—at higher speeds, in heavier traffic, and on more varied terrain.

There are many things you can learn about bike riding only by *doing* it. Still, advice from those with more cycling experience or a different point of view can save you a lot of time, help you learn faster, and keep you from making costly mistakes. And as you learn to ride a bike more efficiently and safely, you'll find that cycling will become more challenging and more fun.

BASIC BIKE-HANDLING

Shifting gears—The gears found on derailleur bicycles vary according to the purposes for which the bike is intended. Racing bikes, for example, come equipped with a relatively narrow range of gears because they're intended for strong, powerful riders. Sport bikes have a broader gearing range to accommodate the fitness levels of a greater variety of riders. Touring and mountain bikes have the widest gearing range of all, to take into account not only a wide variety of riders' abilities, but also mountainous terrain and the possibility of carrying heavy loads.

Most riders know, in some rudimentary way at least, how to go about shifting gears on their bike, and they understand why gears are necessary—they allow a rider to pedal up steep hills that he or she otherwise could not. Most novice riders, however, don't realize the importance of proper *cadence* (pedal revolutions per minute) to comfortable long-distance cycling. Being in the right gear allows you to maintain the proper cadence, enabling you to work at a fairly uniform, efficient level of effort.

For most beginning cyclists, a cadence of 50 or 60 revolutions per minute (rpm) seems most comfortable; that's because this rate is equivalent to a comfortable walking speed. More experienced riders, however, know that 90 to 100 rpm is more efficient. Your leg muscles ultimately get more tired from pushing slowly with more force than they do from pedaling more rapidly with less effort. So it's important, when selecting gears, to pick the one that allows you to maintain the most efficient cadence for the type of terrain you normally ride on. For hills, that's 60 to 80 rpm; for level ground, 80 to 100 rpm; and for downhills, 100 to 120 rpm.

What is meant by the terms *lower* and *higher* gears, anyway? A low gear is one that's relatively easy to pedal in, in which you don't travel very far with each pedal revolution. You're in your lowest gear when the chain is on the small chain ring in front and the large freewheel cog in back. Higher gears, on the other hand, require more effort to pedal but allow you to cover more ground with each pedal stroke. You're in your highest gear when the chain is on the large chain wheel and smallest freewheel cog.

You use low gears when you're starting from a stop, when you're climbing hills, or when you're bucking a head wind. High gears are appropriate for riding fast—on level ground, down a hill, or with a tail wind. For most of the riding you do on level ground, you'll use gears in the middle range. If you're pedaling along and come to a hill, your bike and cadence will begin to slow down, indicating the need to shift to a lower gear.

Probably the biggest mistake new riders make is not anticipating the need to shift down when they approach a hill, *before* it becomes difficult to pedal. Your shifters and derailleurs are among the more fragile of your bike's components, and do not stand up well to abuse. If you find that you've missed the best opportunity to shift, and that your cadence has dropped and you're struggling up a hill, either forget about shifting and stand up to make pedaling easier, or pedal hard for a few strokes and then make your shift, timing it so that you shift at precisely the moment you take pressure off the pedals. The new index-shifting derailleurs are able to shift under a load better than conventional derailleurs, but it's still easier on your drive train if you shift gears at a higher cadence and with less force on the pedals. Remember that your drive train should run silently. If you hear any rubbing or rattling from the chain, adjust the front or rear derailleur until it stops.

Riding a straight line—Ride behind another cyclist and pay attention whether or not he or she rides a straight line. It's surprising how many experienced riders allow their front wheels to wander back and forth as they pedal, wasting energy and potentially endangering any other cyclist riding with them. Learning to ride a straight line, on the other hand, not only enables you to ride more efficiently, but improves your balance and other bike-handling skills as well.

Riding a straight line depends primarily on eye focus and proper body position. At 15 to 20 miles (25 to 30 kilometers) per hour, keep your eyes focused 20 feet (6 meters) ahead. Body position is even more important, and the key to proper body position is to keep your wrists and elbows relaxed, which will allow you to make subtle steering corrections. Keep a

John Lehrer

(Right) Learn how to keep your bike heading in a straight line even when you check behind for traffic. (Below) When applying the brakes hard, make sure your weight is low and to the rear of the bike.

Steve Broaddus

secure but relaxed grip on the handlebars, preferably with your hands on the brake-lever hoods.

The best place to practice riding a straight line is a deserted parking lot or country road. On a road, you can practice riding on the white line marking the shoulder. Start at your normal speed, then speed up and slow way down—you'll find that it's most difficult to ride a straight line at very slow speeds.

Practice until riding a straight line becomes second nature, then learn to ride straight while glancing back over your shoulder, as if you were looking for cars coming up from behind (a situation in which many cyclists swerve into the traffic lane).

Braking—Modern bicycle brakes, whether sidepulls, cantilevers, or the roller-cam and U-brakes found on some mountain bikes, are simple and yet sophisticated—simple because they're cable-actuated mechanical devices whose basic design has varied little over the past several decades, sophisticated because of the degree to which that design has been refined, especially in the past few years. Several years ago, only brakes found in top-of-the-line component groups gave outstanding performance, but that is no longer the case. Now, even the brakes in the second or third lines of a component manufacturer provide high levels of both braking power and control.

If you understand what happens when you apply your brakes, you'll be able to brake more efficiently and avoid getting into trouble. Most of the time when you need to stop, there's no problem because you have plenty of time. But if you find that you're heading into a turn faster than you think is safe, or if you have to avoid an obstacle in your path, you may need to stop faster than anticipated.

In such circumstances, most riders just grab both brake levers and squeeze hard until they start to skid. With that approach, it's easy to lose control of your bike, and the rate of deceleration is less when you're skidding than if the wheels were turning.

When you brake, your body weight shifts from the rear wheel to the front. The harder you brake, the greater the weight on the front wheel and the less the weight on the rear. If you brake too hard, the rear wheel lifts off the pavement and you may pitch over the handlebars.

Because the weight on the front wheel increases as you apply the brakes, the front wheel can take lots of braking force before it starts to skid, but the rear wheel can take only a little. Therefore, in order to slow down quickly, you must apply more force to the front brake lever than to the rear.

You need to apply enough pressure on the front brake to stop your bike,

Be sure you have enough play in your brake levers to give you proper braking control. You should feel the brake pads start to make contact with the rims when the lever has completed about one-third of its travel.

David Madison

If a hill is really steep, it's often easier to take it standing, rocking the bike from side to side and pulling up on the handlebars.

such as a school parking lot on the weekend. Apply the rear brake only hard enough to stop you gently, and learn to apply the front brake harder and harder without increasing the pressure on the rear brake lever too much. If the rear wheel starts to skid, back off on the pressure to the front brake.

Climbing and descending—If you learn to climb hills efficiently, you'll be more comfortable and less tired both at the top of the hill and at the end of your ride. Becoming a good hill climber requires focusing on cadence, developing rhythm, and maintaining momentum.

First, be sure to always select the right gear *before* you hit the hill; when in doubt, pick a slightly lower gear than you think you will need, because you can always shift to a higher gear if you find your rpm is too high. Generally, the most efficient hill-climbing cadence is 60 to 80 rpm.

There are two basic climbing styles—riding in or out of the saddle. Climbing while seated is usually better for less steep grades and on climbs where long, continuous effort is required. Concentrate on maintaining a comfortable, relatively upright posture, with your hands on top of the bars or on the brake hoods; this will allow you to breathe more easily than if you're hunched over the bars. Try to keep a steady, consistent pace; focus on pedaling smoothly. If the hill is long, shifting your weight from the front to the rear of the saddle will make climbing easier.

Climbing a hill while standing requires more agility and upper-body strength. If a hill is steep or if you want to get to the top fast, however, it may be best to stand up for part or most of the climb, because you increase your leverage and power when you stand up. Grip the brake levers and pull up on the bars while pushing down on the pedals; your bike should rock from side to side rhythmically beneath you as you pedal. Depending on the grade, you may need to shift to a higher gear when you stand up in order to maintain the most comfortable cadence.

Even riders who prefer to climb hills while seated often find that

but not enough so that you somersault over the bars. The key is to know how to use the rear brake—if you apply hard pressure to it, at some point it will lock and the wheel will start to skid. The skidding is a signal that the braking effect on the front wheel has begun to make the rear wheel too light. In other words, a skidding *rear* wheel means that the *front* brake is on too hard, and that you need to ease up on it until the rear wheel stops skidding.

Practice your stops on a clear, level area with a good surface that's free from sand, pebbles, and loose dirt,

Steve Broaddus

Steve Broaddus

1. When taking a right-hand curve, start near the center of the road.

2. Then cut in toward the shoulder at the apex of the curve.

3. And exit toward the centerline.

standing out of the saddle occasionally provides a refreshing break, stretching the muscles and making the climb easier.

When you're developing hill-climbing skills, your primary concern is efficiency. Climbing a hill can be drudgery, but descending is the payoff for all the hard work. It's both risky and fun, all the more so the closer you get to the safe maximum speed.

But descending means greater speed, which creates several problems, among them the need to allow for greater braking distances and the danger of taking curves too fast.

When you're descending, part of your braking effort is required just to prevent you from going any faster, so you have to begin braking at a distance from the place you want to stop that is greater than if you were riding on level ground. To practice descending, pick a specific route that you can ride several times a week if possible, a little faster each time. By riding the same course, you'll be able to gauge your progress better. Use the same rules for braking that you do on level ground: a skidding rear wheel indicates that you're putting too much pressure on the front brake.

Cornering—Learning to take corners, especially on descents, also requires practice. The important factor is how much you can safely lean into the turn. This is determined by the condition of the road surface and the degree to which it is banked. You can't change the road, but you can control your speed and the path you take through the curve (called "the line"). Again, you must practice this skill again and again, each time altering your speed, the line you take through the curve, and the amount you lean your bike.

For maximum control when cornering, stay low on your bike with your back nearly horizontal, your elbows bent but relaxed, and your hands down in the "drops" with two fingers on each brake lever. For a right-hand curve, start close to the centerline, cut toward the shoulder, then exit the curve toward the centerline. For a left-hand curve, start close to the edge of the road, cut in toward the center and exit toward the edge of the road. Once you pick a line, don't alter it when you're in the corner or you greatly increase the risk of losing control.

Whether you're taking a corner while descending or on level ground,

Steve Broaddus

you should brake *before* you reach the apex of the corner, not while you're in it. If you grab the front brake in the middle of a turn, the front wheel can skid or lock up—especially if the road is bumpy, wet, or covered with loose gravel—which can cause you to fall. Also, be sure to keep your inside pedal up as you round a corner, because if the pedal catches the ground it could lift the bike, causing you to crash.

Rules of the road—Many adults have avoided cycling because they dislike riding in traffic and think it's too dangerous. Perhaps they rode bikes as kids, when the roads were less congested, and they really might want to get back on a bike now. A little voice inside them says: "Riding a bike is fun! It feels good!"

But a bigger, responsible "adult" voice also says: "It's dangerous! Look at all those cars on the road—I could get killed!" And inside most of these would-be cyclists is the voice of the motorist they've become that makes them aware of how they feel when *they're* behind the wheel and see somebody riding a bicycle. They probably get nervous, because they know that driving a car is a risky activity, and they know that bicycle riders are even more vulnerable and fragile. And, as motorists, they probably also have the feeling, no matter how vague, that the roads belong to the cars. So they can't imagine themselves, as adults, riding a bicycle regularly. And the "reasons" they create for not riding are those that "prove" that riding a bicycle on the roads is too dangerous.

If you live in a city, you have to learn how to deal with riding in traffic. To do so, you have to improve your riding skills, which in turn bolsters your confidence in your ability to ride safely. But it also helps immensely if you're sure both what is legally required of you as a cyclist, and the kinds of situations you're likely to encounter when riding in the city.

In order to deal with riding in traffic, you need to have a plan:

1. *Make sure your bike is in good repair*. You can't relax on your bike if you're worried that your brakes won't stop you or if you're always being distracted by a squeaky chain. Take your bike to a shop regularly for maintenance; better yet, read the chapter in this book (and read other books) on bike maintenance, and learn to do some of it yourself.

Sidewalks are almost always for pedestrians only.

2. *Perfect your bike-handling skills.* Practice the skills and techniques mentioned so far in this chapter.

3. *Consider yourself a vehicle and obey essentially the same rules of the road that you would if you were driving a car.* Here's some information on cycling accidents, not to frighten you, but to enlighten you. After all, you need to know the real dangers you face out there on the road, not just what you imagine the dangers to be:

(a) Although cyclists (especially inexperienced ones) worry most about car-bike collisions, in fact they account for only about 12 percent of all cycling accidents. And in most car-bike accidents, the bicycle rider does something illegal or unusual to cause the accident.

(b) New cyclists most fear being hit from behind by a car overtaking them. In reality, this accounts for less than 5 percent of cycling accidents (but about 40 percent of the fatalities.)

(c) Cycle-commuting to work in traffic is among the safest of all cycling activities.

(d) Most cycling accidents happen to young or relatively inexperienced riders. The most important factor in reducing the number of cycling accidents is improving your riding skills.

Learning how to avoid accidents depends on how well you ride the thin line between thinking like a motorist and asserting your rights as a cyclist. In many ways, safe riding is a matter of attitude. In practice, cyclists fare better when they regard themselves as vehicles, which means among other things: ride on the right side of the street; yield to crossing traffic when you reach a road more prominent than the one you're riding on; yield to traffic already in the lane into which you intend to move.

But treating yourself as a vehicle also means giving up what some cyclists regard as their "special privileges": running stop signs and stop lights, and making turns from the wrong places on the street.

Riding a bicycle as a vehicle requires learning and practicing new procedures, too, such as positioning yourself correctly in a lane of traffic and knowing how to approach an intersection. This sometimes involves unlearning rules you may have learned as a child. For example, it's *not* generally safest to ride right next to the curb. Rather, it's better to move out closer to traffic, where you can be seen more easily. On wide roads, ride just outside the traffic lane, about three feet to the right of cars. On narrow roads, ride just inside the traffic lane, so that cars can pass you by moving over slightly. On a street where there are parked cars, maintain an even distance just to the left of them—don't duck toward the curb and weave around them; this makes it

harder for moving cars to see you. (For a more detailed discussion of riding in traffic, see John Forester's excellent book, *Effective Cycling*.)

That's the practical aspect of regarding yourself as a vehicle when you ride your bike. The attitudinal aspect is less obvious, and can be succinctly stated as follows: Don't be a wimp. In other words, recognize that as a cyclist you have an equal right to the use of the road. And paradoxically, it's because cyclists are so much more vulnerable and fragile than motorists that it's necessary to be assertive about your right to use the road along with the cars.

If you want to be treated as a person with equal rights, you have to act that way. In the case of your right to use the road, the law will back you up in almost every case. But if you don't believe you have a right to be on the road — if you have cyclist inferiority complex—then you'll ride anxiously rather than confidently.

Cars are a fact of life, but studies prove that coexistence is possible. The proper attitude is to ride courageously and defensively, but not fearfully. Be careful, practice, and pay attention to what you're doing when you throw a leg over the top tube.

Remember, the more proficient a rider you become, the less likely you are to have an accident.

When you're on your bike, consider yourself a vehicle. It's the safest course of action, and it's usually the law, as well.

IMPROVING YOUR PEDALING TECHNIQUE

Two differences in pedaling technique set proficient cyclists apart from novice riders: the ability to acheive proper cadence (pedaling rate) and increased power output. Along with correct bike fit and posture, these are the four keys to efficient cycling.

As stated at the beginning of the chapter, most beginning cyclists feel that pedaling 50 to 60 rpm is the most efficient way to ride because that's about the "cadence" that most humans walk. Proficient cyclists, however, know that pedaling the bicycle rapidly at 90 to 100 rpm (called "spinning") is actually more efficient over long distances.

If you pedal slowly up a hill in a high gear, using a great deal of force with each pedal stroke, it's more tiring than pedaling rapidly in a low gear, although you're performing the same amount of work. This is because powering your way up the hill relies primarily on strength and is likely to become anaerobic, while using a faster cadence is a low-output, high repetition form of exercise relying on coordination, technique, and aerobic capacity—a form of work that can be continued over a longer period of time before fatigue sets in. The other major advantage of spinning is that it's less stressful on a cyclist's knee joints.

The best way to increase your cadence is gradually; any drastic change is going to feel awkward and inefficient. First, find the cadence you

David Madison

Proper pedaling technique will make you a more efficient cyclist, and a fitter one, as well.

prefer by riding on a flat stretch, timing your pedal revolutions for fifteen seconds and multiplying by four.

Let's assume you discover that your cadence on level ground in a particular gear is 72. To increase your cadence, shift your bike into the next lower gear, which should result in an 8 to 10 percent increase in your pedaling speed. Give yourself a few weeks to get accustomed to this more rapid cadence, then shift one gear lower. Check your cadence every few weeks until it hits the 90 to 100 mark.

Once you're comfortable pedaling at 90 rpm, you can begin to work on increasing the length of your power stroke. In order to do so, you need to be riding with cleated cycling shoes (including the clipless/strapless variety); you can't apply power through the rearward and upward portion of the pedal stroke without being securely attached to the pedals.

If you extend the length of the power portion of your pedal stroke, you'll make use of more leg muscles than if you only apply power through a limited range. Novice riders simply push the pedals down with their quadriceps (upper thigh). If you pull back and upward on the pedal with the hamstrings (back of the thigh) and gluteal (butt) muscles, you can maximize the force applied to each revolution of the pedals.

Increasing the length of the power stroke, like increasing cadence, must be done gradually. Most beginning riders only apply power through about 90 degrees of the pedal circle, typically from the two o'clock to the five o'clock position. If this description fits the way you pedal, try gradually applying power through the six o'clock and seven o'clock positions. Just don't expect to be able to apply a uniform amount of force throughout the pedal stroke.

It's hard to incorporate these (or any other) changes into your riding style and still have fun cycling if you focus on them continuously. The key is to divide your rides into three parts: On the first section, warm up gradually and don't worry about technique; in the second portion, concentrate on improving one aspect of your technique; on the last third of your ride, enjoy yourself.

RIDING FOR FITNESS AND COMPETITION

Many people are content to ride their bikes at a comfortable pace a couple of times a week for ten to fifteen miles (fifteen to twenty five kilometers) at a time, but some riders want more. They're serious about fitness, and for them a bicycle is a means of achieving it. For these cyclists, riding becomes *training*, and they begin keeping diaries and thinking about the competitive side of cycling.

A bicycle is an excellent year-round training device—you can use it to lose weight, increase your physical energy and mental alertness, improve your muscle tone, reduce stress and illness, and develop a strong cardiovascular system.

There are two basic kinds of training: *long, steady distance*, which develops endurance, and *interval workouts*, which develop power and speed. Once you've accustomed your body to riding several times a week, your first priority in becoming fit should be to establish a *mileage base*, consisting of moderately intense, steady riding done four or five times a week for one to two hours at a time.

The only real differences between this type of training and general recreational riding are that distance training is *systematic* and *goal-oriented*. Each ride is planned—you decide to ride a specific distance or unit of time—and fits into a larger "plan," a weekly, monthly, or seasonal training program. If your goal is to improve your fitness, it should be reflected in the program. Over a series of weeks, you gradually increase your mileage, improve your average speed, or both. If your goal is to maintain your present level of fitness, your training schedule should reflect that, too.

Besides the considerations of time and distance, *long, steady riding* focuses on pedal cadence—your goal is to ride fast enough to produce a *training effect*, or improve your cardiovascular system. This means that you must strive for a cadence of 90 to 100 rpm in a gear large enough to elevate your heart rate to about 75 percent of its maximum. (A rough formula for determining maximum heart rate is to subtract your age from 210.) For most fit riders, this means that your heart rate should reach 140–160 beats per minute. At first, you can take your pulse once or twice during your rides, but after a while you should be able to tell when you're getting a sufficient workout.

Interval workouts are shorter than long, steady distance sessions but are much more stressful. Before attempting to add intervals to a training program, a rider should have at least a 1500-mile (2400-kilometer) foundation of long, steady distance. Then, for the first month, no more than one session of intervals per week should be attempted; in the second month, one more can be added, provided that the rider allows at least two recovery days of steady distance riding in between.

The purpose of interval workouts is to develop speed and power by sim-

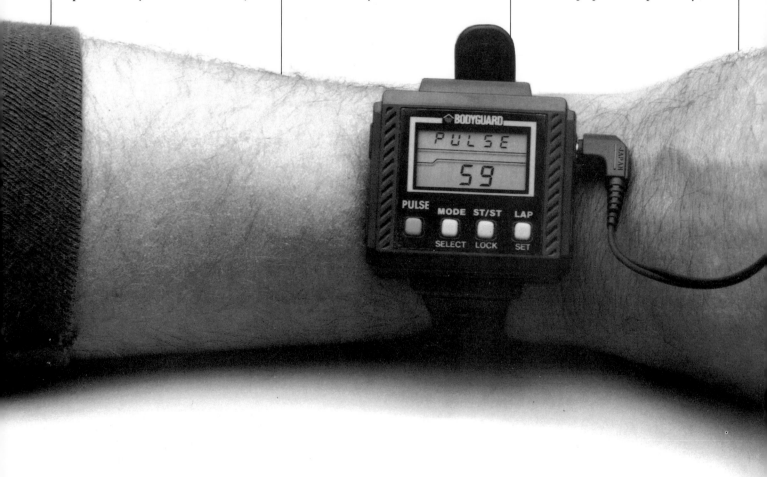

John Lehrer

ulating the intensity of high-speed racing for short periods of time, typically a minute. After warming up sufficiently, a rider might shift into a moderately high gear and ride for a minute at nearly all-out effort, then shift to a lower gear and pedal easily for a minute, go hard again for a minute, and so on, up to ten repetitions.

The idea is to strive to put the same effort into each hard interval (a cyc-

ling computer helps here). After ten repetitions, you should ride along at a steady speed for fifteen to twenty minutes to flush lactic acid and other toxins from your muscles. There are many variations of intervals—the intensity of effort, length of the interval, the number of repetitions all can change. For more information on the subject, consult books or magazine articles on training for bicycle racing.

Riding fast (above) is good exercise and fun, too. Keeping track of your pulse will maximize the benefits of your workouts.

TRAINING AIDS

To achieve improved fitness through cycling, it helps to develop a training program, establish regular training routes, and keep a training log.

Training program—To keep improving (and to prevent overtraining and injury), you should have a plan directed toward a specific goal. For example, you might want to ride 50 or 100 miles (80 or 160 kilometers). A training program is the best way to achieve such a goal.

Training routes—It's better to establish several regular training routes instead of "just going out to ride." That way, it's easier to set and meet specific riding goals. Also, riding a familiar route gives you impetus to continue when you feel stale and the going gets tough. If possible, plan the courses for your training rides several miles from your house, so you can ride to them for your warm-up. Your routes should have relatively few interruptions (stop lights, traffic); other than that, vary them in terms of distance, terrain, and so on.

Training log—Recording your workouts is a way to find out what sort of training is effective for you and what isn't. Your training log should give at least the distances, times, and types of courses you ride, plus the degree of effort and how you feel while riding. Take your resting pulse immediately upon arising to see whether you're overtraining. If it's ten beats above normal, it's probably time to back off.

John Lehrer

Steve Broaddus

WEEK	MON	TUE	WED	THU	FRI	SAT	SUN	TOTALS		
1	5	10	15	REST	10	30	10	80	M	
2	10	10	15	REST	10	35	10	90	I	
3	10	10	15	REST	10	40	10	95	L	
4	10	15	5	REST	10	45	10	105	E	
5	10	15	20	REST	10	50	15	120	A	
6	10	15	20	REST	15	55	15	130	G	
7	15	15	20	REST	15	60	15	140	E	
8	15	15	25	REST	15	65	15	150		
9	15	15	25	REST	15	70	20	160		
10	15	15	25	REST	10	5	100	170		

SPECIFIC FITNESS GOALS

Setting and working toward specific cycling goals makes it easier to maintain the habit of fitness. A cherished goal of many new cyclists is to ride a century (160 kilometers). If you're presently riding about fifty miles (80 kilometers) a week in three rides, you can train to complete a century in ten to twelve weeks.

The key is doing one long weekend ride, and riding almost every other day. The chart at the left shows what a ten-week training schedule might look like.

The idea is to increase the weekly distance by about 10 percent, to get in a rest day and to use easy-to-deal-with five-mile (8-kilometer) increments. It's best to ride the sort of terrain in practice that you'll be riding during the century. If possible, practice on the course.

David Madison

Organized rides and races provide competitive incentive to fitness-oriented cyclists.

GETTING STARTED IN COMPETITION

Riding for fitness may not be enough for you, especially if you've seen television coverage of the Tour de France or Paris Roubaix. Bicycle racing is an exciting, demanding sport that requires not only cardiovascular fitness, but a high degree of coordination, balance, and quickness, plus a mastery of racing strategy and technique. If being in the midst of a swarming pack of riders unnerves you a bit, however, there's a less risky way to get started in competitive cycling: riding time trials.

Time trials are a great competitive first step; there's virtually no danger of crashing because you'll be riding alone, and you can ride as hard as you wish. What's more, there's a good chance you'll find a time-trials series being held near where you live; if not, it's easy to organize one through a local bike shop or cycling club.

A time trial is sometimes called "the race of truth" because it's just you against the clock; the only tactic is to pace yourself to ride as fast as you can over a given distance. Time trials can be any length, but they are usually five to ten miles (eight to sixteen kilometers), a distance that people of all ages and abilities can handle. There are several ways to "win" in time trials, too; you can place yourself relative to other riders or teams, or you can set a personal best. In fact, the main goal is personal improvement.

The ingredients for a successful time trial are simple: a group of riders, a measured stretch of road, and someone with a stopwatch, a paper, and pencil. The competitors ride out to a specific point (usually starting at one-minute intervals), turn around and return (or they ride a loop course).

A number of things will help you ride time trials well. It goes without saying that the better physical condition you're in, the better you'll fare.

It's also very important to warm up properly, to get your blood circulating and loosen up your muscles. Stretch your muscles, pedal easily, and throw in a few hard, short sprints. Warm up for at least a half-hour; for the final ten minutes (until just before it's your time to start), ride around easily.

When you roll up to the start, put your bike in a gear that's about two gears lower than your cruising gear. Be sure that your toe straps are snug. The timer will let you know how many seconds to the start, and a

David B. Keith

holder will keep your bike in place. Take a couple of deep breaths before you start. Take off standing up and pedal until you need to shift to a higher gear. Then sit down, shift, stand up, and pedal hard again. The idea is to accelerate as rapidly as possible to the speed you want to maintain.

It's important to concentrate both on the terrain and how your body is working during a time trial. You won't be allowed to draft (stay in the slipstream of the rider ahead of you), so you must immediately pass anyone you catch. The only real bike-handling skills required are in making a quick turnaround at the halfway point, if the course is an out-and-back.

As you approach the turnaround, shift into a slightly lower gear to anticipate the turn, concentrate on the marker or cone, watch for traffic and other cyclists, make your turn, and get back up to cruising speed as soon as possible.

In the last half of the time trial, concentrate especially hard on your form and the effort you're putting out. Try to ride progressively harder, but save most of your energy for the last mile, where you should go all-out. After the finish, even though it may be tempting to get off your bike and rest, ride easily for fifteen minutes in a low gear to cool down.

Time trials are enjoyable and rewarding. They're good as a speed workout, they keep you from getting mentally and physically stale, and they're a good gauge of whether your training program is working.

Bike Maintenance

Bicycles are beautiful and simple machines, yet most riders don't know much about taking care of them. Learning the basics of bicycle maintenance is fairly easy, however, and pays dividends in a number of ways, perhaps the least of which is financial. In the first place, if you understand how your bike works and how to perform minor repairs, you'll be able to ride with peace of mind; you won't be afraid that you'll break down and become stranded. That means you'll ride more frequently and farther, and become a more proficient cyclist.

Also, if you care for your bike yourself, you'll take more pride in its appearance and keep it in better repair. You'll learn how to perform preventive maintenance, which will help your bike's components last longer. Your confidence in dealing with all things mechanical will improve. Of course, you'll save money by performing your own routine maintenance, too.

This chapter introduces you to the basics of bike maintenance—to let you know the procedures you need to learn and the tools you need to acquire to keep your bicycle in fine working order. We'll begin with the simplest, most frequently performed tasks. If you're not used to using a screwdriver or an Allen wrench, making minor repairs and adjustments might seem like a tall order, but your biggest investment will be time and patience. This chapter is an introduction, not a comprehensive treatise on maintenance. For more information, buy a good book on bicycle repairs. Two of the best are *Anybody's Bike Book* by Tom Cuthbertson and *Richard's Bicycle Book* by Richard Ballantine. Both are available in paperback, both have been revised recently, and both feature clear explanations and helpful illustrations.

Let's begin by assuming that you've just brought your beautiful, shiny new bike home from the shop and that you can't wait to go for a ride. Well, you're in luck. If the mechanics at your bike shop have adjusted your bike properly, you've got as much as a month's worth of riding before your bike will need anything except a chain lubing and wipe-down; so you've got plenty of time to learn basic maintenance procedures.

Nearly all bike-maintenance tasks fall into one or more of these four categories: cleaning, lubrication, adjustment, and repair. Some tasks are simple, some are more complex; some need to be done every time you go for a ride, others only need to be performed once a year. The good news is that those maintenance procedures you'll need to do most frequently are also the simplest.

PROPER TOOLS

Bicycle maintenance and repair requires the right tools. First, let's consider the tools you'll need to take with you on your rides. For normal, everyday riding, everything you need can be carried easily within the main triangle of your bike frame and in a small under-the-seat pack:

Frame Pump—It should fit snugly along the seat tube or under the top tube of your bike. Don't use it to pump up your tires everyday; use a floor pump for that, and use the frame pump for flat tires on the road.

Patch kit—Usually comes in a small plastic box; keep it stocked with three or four patches, and don't let the cement get dried up. You might want

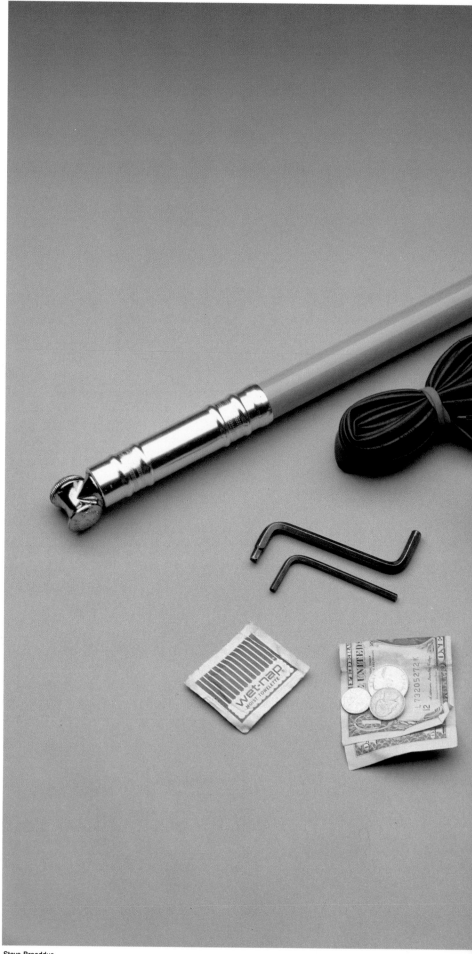

Steve Broaddus

to include a small section (1" × ½") of old tire casing or a patch from a motorcycle-tube patch kit in case you need to patch a severely cut tire.

Tire irons—The best are made from plastic, and are used to pry the tire off the rim. These often come in sets of three, but you can get by with two.

Spare tube—Occasionally, you'll get a flat that damages the tube in your tire beyond repair, so carry an extra. Coat it with talcum powder so that it slips into the tire more easily, then wrap it in a small plastic bag.

Allen wrenches—Most likely, you'll need 4-, 5- and 6mm wrenches.

Screwdriver—A small flat-blade or Phillips-head model is useful for derailleur adjustments and other odd jobs. *Don't* use it as a substitute for a tire iron, though.

Towelette—The moist kind wrapped in aluminum foil will get your hands "deep-down clean."

You also might want to carry along some money (for on-the-road nourishment and emergency phone calls), a local street map, lip balm, a small adjustable wrench (necessary, not optional, if your bike has axle nuts), a spoke wrench, small pocket knife, aspirin, and a Presta valve adapter. All of these items are inexpensive; they should total no more than $40, a small price to pay for peace of mind on the road.

All the tools you'll need 99 percent of the time you break down on the road. Clockwise from 12 o'clock: a frame pump, under-the-seat bag, map, patch kit, Var tire lever, valve adapter, screwdriver, small adjustable wrench, money, towlette, Allen wrenches, spare tube, and talc.

Fixing a flat:

1. When removing a rear wheel, stand the bike "on its nose."

2. Get the first lever under the tire bead without pinching the tube.

3. Insert a second lever a few inches from the first.

4. After unseating the entire bead on one side of the tire, carefully remove the tube.

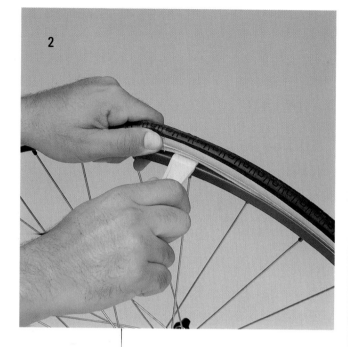

2

Steve Broaddus

1

Steve Broaddus

ROADSIDE REPAIRS

By far, the most common repair you'll need to make while you're riding is fixing a flat tire. No matter how careful you are, every so often you'll hear that dreaded p-s-s-s-s-s-s! sound signaling you to pull off the road to take a tire-repair break.

Find a safe, comfortable place to stop your bike, preferably near a fence, tree, or other object to lean your bike against while you repair the flat tire. Most flat tires result from thorns, tacks, shards of metal, and broken glass. Try to find what caused the flat—inspect the tire surface carefully to locate it. If you can find the object, remove it, and make a mental note of its position so that you can more easily find the hole in the tube.

Next, remove the wheel. Do *not* turn the bike upside down to perform this operation. You'll likely scratch up your seat and bend your brake-cable housing if you do. If the flat tire is on the rear wheel (and it usually is), shift the chain to the smallest chain wheel and freewheel cog to release

3

Steve Broaddus

4

Steve Broaddus

derailleur spring tension and make it easier to remove the wheel. The best way to remove the rear wheel is to rest the bike "nose first" on the side of the front wheel and the handlebars, with the rear wheel up in the air at chest level, where it's easier to work on. Release the quick-release lever on the rear brake so the wheel will clear the brake pads easily, open the quick-release wheel skewer, and pull the rear derailleur body down and back; the wheel should drop out easily. Lean the rear end of the bike against a tree or sign post, or lay it carefully down on its left side (*not* the derailleur side). If your front tire is flat, simply release the front brake and wheel skewer, take the wheel out and carefully lay the bike down.

When you've removed the wheel, it's time to patch or replace the tube. To do this, you must remove the tire bead from one side of the rim, remove the tube, patch or replace it, reinsert it, reseat the tire, then reinflate it. The tire bead is the stretch-resistant cord around the edge of the tire that makes contact with the rim; it hooks under the edge of the rim when you inflate the tire, keeping the

air pressure from blowing the tire off the rim.

To unseat the tire bead, you need to insert tire levers under the bead and pry it up and over the edge of the rim. Start somewhere on the rim that is at least twelve inches from the valve stem. Be careful not to pinch the tube while you are unseating the tire bead; plastic tire levers are less likely to pinch the tube (thus creating another hole) than are metal tire irons. To prevent pinching the tube, carefully work the lever in just far enough to catch the bead, then slide the lever up the inside of the casing. When you pry the bead out at one point, hold it over the edge of the rim, leaving the tire lever inserted under the bead. If the lever has a small notch on the opposite end, hook it around a spoke to hold it in place. Otherwise, just hold on to it and pry out another section of bead about three inches from the first. Do this once more (using a third lever or by withdrawing one of the two already used). At this point, enough of the tire has generally been pried over the edge of the rim so that you can pull out all the levers, then slide one lever all around the

edge of the tire, unseating it completely from the rim.

Next, reach inside the tire and carefully pull the tube out, making sure not to dislodge or damage the rim strip. (If your bike comes equipped with a rubber rim strip, by the way, replace it with nylon-filament strapping tape when you get home. Rubber rim strips are the source of many flats because they move around on the inside of the rim, exposing the inner tube to the sharp space ends. Now you must either patch the tube or replace it with a spare. If you decide to patch it, and if you were able to discern the cause of the flat, try to remember where the hole in the tube might be in relation to the valve stem on the tire. With your pump, inflate the tube to about twice its normal size (it won't pop). Hold the tube close to your face so that you can feel or hear the air escaping from the puncture. If the hole is very small, you might have to dunk the tube in water or moisten a section of it with saliva to look for bubbles or listen for escaping air.

When you've located the hole, take the small piece of sandpaper in your

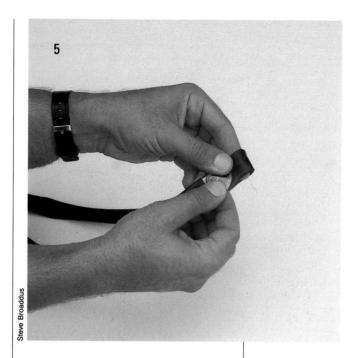

Steve Broaddus

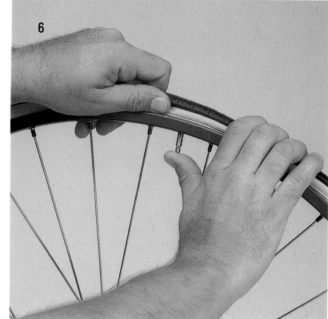

Steve Broaddus

5. Press the patch firmly on the glue; when it has dried it should no longer be shiny.

6. Reseat the tire, beginning at the valve. You may need to press the valve stem up into the tire with your thumb in order to ensure proper reseating.

7. Carefully push the tube into the tire with your fingers, followed by tucking the bead behind the rim with your thumb.

8. Try to get the last bit of tire over the edge of the rim with your thumbs; if that doesn't work, use a tire lever very carefully.

9. Before each ride, inflate your tires to full pressure with a floor pump. This will minimize the chance of a flat and maximize tire life.

patch kit and roughen up the surface of the tube around the hole. Next, spread a thin layer of glue in a circular pattern on the tube, with the hole at its center. (It should be larger than the patch you'll use.) Peel the aluminum foil off the back of a patch and put a little glue around the edges. When the shiny glue has become dull, it's dry enough to apply the patch; this should only take a couple of minutes. Press the patch tightly to the tube, concentrating on the edges. (You can leave the cellophane on the front of the patch; it will keep any excess glue from discoloring the sidewall of the tire.)

After a few minutes, inflate the tube to slightly larger than normal size to make sure that the patch holds and that there are no other holes in the tube. Now it's time to reinsert the tube into the tire. Before you do, feel around the inside of the tire carefully to make sure no sharp objects are protruding through the casing. The last thing you'll want to do is to reinflate the tire, only to have it go flat from a thorn or sliver of glass that you weren't aware of!

Inflate the tube just enough to give it some shape, then reinsert it begin-

ning with the valve, pushing the tube into the tire as far as it will go. Distribute the tube evenly, and be careful not to twist it. Now it's time to work the bead back under the lip of the rim. There are three important considerations here: First, the bead must go back under the rim without catching the tube in between itself and the rim, thereby creating another puncture. Second, the bead has to be evenly and completely seated, so that when you inflate the tire, it doesn't blow off the rim. Third, you don't want to pinch the tube with a tire iron, so you'll reinsert it only with your hands.

Sit down, placing the wheel in your lap with the valve hole at the twelve o'clock position, in front of your face. Begin reseating the tire at the valve. Lift the bead over the rim and reinsert it behind the rim's edge. Work with both hands, moving around the tire in both directions away from the valve stem. Make sure you're not pinching the tube between the rim and the tire as you reseat the bead. As you get more and more tire under the rim, the task will become more difficult. Try to get the last section of tire over the edge of the rim by pressing hard with your thumbs. As a last resort (and

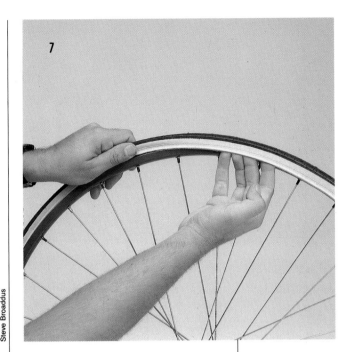

Steve Broaddus

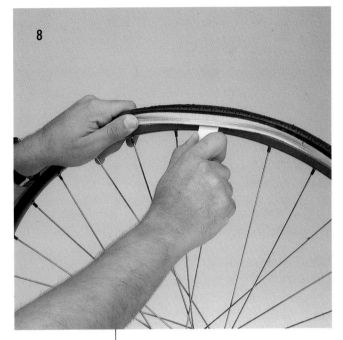

Steve Broaddus

this is unavoidable with some narrow, high-pressure clinchers), carefully pry it over with a tire lever. Before you reinflate the tire, push the valve stem into the tire to be sure the bead is seated at that point; sometimes the thick rubber at the base of the valve stem gets wedged in between the tire bead and the rim.

Inflate the tire until it feels full but soft, then inspect the tire where it meets the rim on both sides of the wheel, to be sure that no parts of the bead are creeping out from behind the edge of the rim. Make sure that the tire is evenly seated, with no bulges. Then inflate the tire fully, bracing the wheel against a tree or sign post as you pump. Rotate the wheel so that the valve is at its highest point (twelve o'clock), push the pump head onto the valve, wrap your left hand around the pump head (for right handers), with your thumb around the rim and tire. Hold the pump head perpendicular to the valve stem throughout the pumping stroke; don't rock it from side to side or you'll let air out and possibly damage the valve stem. Brace the bottom of the wheel against the ground with your left foot so it won't move around; you may need to

lean into the stroke with your whole body as the tire becomes nearly fully inflated, bracing the pump handle against your knee.

When the tire is as hard as you can get it (most hand pumps are good only for 100 pounds [45 kilograms] of pressure), strike the pump head with your fist to remove it from the valve. Be sure to screw the Presta valve closed, reinstall the wheel, close the quick-release on your brake caliper, and you're ready to roll.

Fortunately, when you break down on the road, ninety-nine times out of a hundred it's because of a flat tire, and once you learn to fix a flat (it takes about a half-dozen tries to become proficient), it's a snap.

Once they're tightened and adjusted, most parts of a bicycle stay that way for a long time. The only other roadside repairs are minor derailleur or brake adjustments (a cable might come loose), or tightening the bolt in your handlebar stem or seat post. Mechanical problems that are more serious (a bent wheel or derailleur broken in an accident, for instance) will probably completely disable your bike, even if you're an experienced mechanic.

Steve Broaddus

REGULAR HOME MAINTENANCE

Proper routine maintenance of your bicycle means keeping it clean, and keeping all of its component parts tight, corrosion-free, and adjusted. Keeping your bike in good working order only requires an hour a week at most, even if you ride everyday. As is the case with maintenance on the road, you need the right tools. Some of these are special-purpose tools, and some you probably have around the house already. Buy good-quality tools, the kind with guarantees against breakage. You don't have to acquire your bike tools all at once—some can wait, because you won't use them right away or very often, or because they require more experience than what's needed for general maintenance.

Here's what you'll need for most general maintenance and repair on your bike:

Screwdrivers—A couple of small-to-medium Phillips and flat-blade models.

Allen wrenches—Typically 3, 4, 5 and 6 millimeters.

Pliers—Needle-nose.

Open-end or box-end wrenches—Typically 8, 9, 10, 12 and 15 millimeters. An 8-9-10 millimeter "Y" wrench will work fine for most bikes built in the 1980s; a 4- or 6-inch (10- or 15-centimeter) adjustable wrench will fit most odd sizes. Check your bike's requirements; more bikes these days are using Allen-head bolts on brakes and derailleurs.

Blackburn

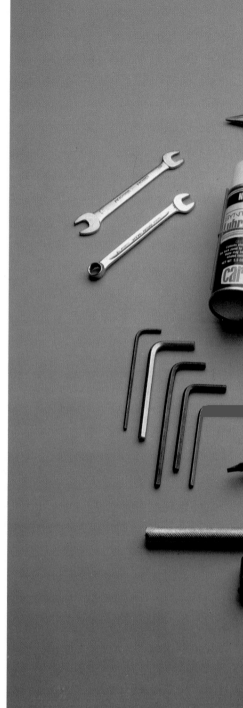

A workstand and the proper tools, plus a little careful study and experience, make home maintenance a relatively simple job. Clockwise from upper left: open-end wrenches, lubricant, needle-nose pliers, chain tool, freewheel remover, cable cutters, spoke wrench, large adjustable wrench, headset and bottom bracket tools, cone wrenches, crank tools, screwdriver, grease, ratchet and sockets, Allen wrenches, and a "Y" wrench.

Floor pump—You'll need this to pump up high-pressure tires before every ride. A floor pump is the only way to do it safely, dependably, and easily. Silca and Zefal make the best floor pumps; be sure to get one with a gauge on it.

Chain-removal tool—Inexpensive, indispensable, and available at your bike shop.

Freewheel remover—Be sure it fits your freewheel.

Cable cutters—Pliers just don't make it; they mash cable threads and make an awful mess of things.

Work stand—Expensive ($50–$150) but worth it. To work on your bike, you have to suspend it off the ground, preferably at waist level, so you can freely turn the cranks and wheels. (Wind trainers can be used as makeshift work stands.)

Solvents and lubricants—Solvents to clean the grease and grime off components, lubricants to keep clean components slippery and squeak-free. Kerosene, carburetor cleaner, or paint thinner will work as a solvent. High-temperature, water-dispersing bearing grease will keep bolt threads, cables and bearings lubricated; an aerosol chain lube or medium-weight machine oil are fine for your bicycle's chain and other small moving parts that require lubrication.

These tools will enable you to adjust and dismantle the brakes, derailleurs, shift levers, stem, handlebars, chain rings, and chain.

BASIC PROCEDURES

Three aspects of bike upkeep require continuous attention, and comprise about 75 percent of the time you'll spend on maintenance: keeping your bike clean, tire maintenance, and chain care.

To begin, if you keep your bike clean, you'll be way ahead of the game as far as bike maintenance is concerned. In what seems like no time at all, a shiny new bike can become covered with dirt and grime—especially a mountain bike, or a bike that's ridden regularly in rainy weather. The problem is more than one of appearances—putting up with a layer of filth on your bike. The components on a bike that are not kept clean collect grit, and as a result come out of adjustment and wear out faster. Also, it's easier and more pleasant to perform routine maintenance on a clean bike. Bicycle cleanliness, in other words, is an important first step of preventive maintenance.

The best way to keep your bike clean is not to let it get dirty in the first place. In other words, instead of waiting until your bike gets really filthy to clean it, after every ride, take a clean, damp cloth and a spray bottle of an all-purpose household cleaner and go over your bike—the frame, the wheels, the brakes, the handlebars, the cables, the seat post—everywhere except the chain. Use a soft, nylon brush to remove really stubborn grease deposits. Be careful not to scratch the paint, and look closely for greasy residue around the brakes and derailleurs, and under the head-

Steve Broaddus

(Left) Spend a little time after every few rides keeping the grime and dirt off your bike—it's much easier to keep it clean that way. (Above) Apart from keeping your tires inflated, lubing your chain is the most frequent task you should perform.

set and bottom bracket. Use an old, dirty rag to clean the excess oil and accumulated grit off the chain. Just spray the chain lightly with chain lube, hold a towel around it, and run the pedals backward. Wipe off the chain rings and clean the freewheel cogs by inserting a folded rag between the cogs and turning the freewheel. Do the same on the jockey pulleys of the derailleur. If you don't perform this light clean-up every couple of rides, after just a few months of riding you can look forward to a five-hour minor overhaul—in which you have to remove most of the bike's components—to accomplish the same thing.

You can eliminate many on-the-road tire problems with a few simple at-home tire maintenance tricks, the most important of which is *keeping your tires properly inflated.* Lightweight bicycle tires lose three to four pounds (one to two kilograms) of air a day, so inflate them before every ride, using a floor pump with a built-in gauge. The recommended pressure will be marked on the tire's side-

wall. If your tires are underinflated, there's a greater chance they'll blow out if you hit a bump or pothole, because the tire will bottom out and pinch the tube against the rim. You run a greater risk of rim damage with underinflated tires, too.

Check the condition of your tires before each ride by visually inspecting the tread and sidewall for cuts. If you find a cut in the casing that allows the inner tube to protrude, replace the tire. Inspecting your tires regularly will allow you to evaluate tread wear, which is important for protection against flats. Lightweight, wired-on tires will usually last about 1000 miles (1600 kilometers) on a rear wheel, and 2000 (3200 kilometers) miles on a front wheel. If you get a couple of flats in succession in a worn tire, that's a sign that there's not much rubber between the inner tube and the road, and you're better off to pitch the tire than risk a serious, unrepairable blowout.

Besides keeping good rubber on your rims, the best way to prevent flats is to wipe your tires with the palm of your gloved hand every time you hear yourself passing through debris on the road that might be broken glass, thorns, and so on. Lightly touching your glove to the tire while you're moving will usually knock sharp objects loose before they have a chance to work through the tire to the tube. Of course, it's also a good idea to pay close attention to where you ride on the road, taking care not to ride too close to the curb, where most of the litter winds up. And be careful not to get your hand caught in the spokes!

Some relatively new products drastically reduce the chance of flats, such as tires with Kevlar belting under the tread; tougher, polyurethane tubes; and lightweight, puncture-resistant plastic strips known as tire liners.

The final item on your bike requiring regular attention is your chain. Because it's made up of hundreds of tiny, interconnected moving parts, it needs to be lubricated regularly in order to work properly. Unfortunately, the lubrication (usually some form of petroleum-based liquid, such as machine oil or an aerosol chain lube) attracts dirt, creating a layer of gritty gunk that adheres to your chain, your clothes and your body, should you come in contact with it.

So it's important to keep your chain lubed, but clean. This means to lube it frequently and to apply the correct amount (and type) of lubrication. Assuming that you ride four to six times per week, ten to thirty miles (sixteen to forty eight kilometers) per ride, lube your chain once every week. If you ride in the rain or in especially dusty conditions, clean and lubricate it more often. Wipe the chain clean, then apply an even coat of lubricant. Use a lightweight machine oil (applied from a mechanic's pump can) or an aerosol chain lube (not a product like WD-40, which is too lightweight to stay in place) to lube the chain. Lay the oil on the cylindrical rollers. Let it soak in for ten minutes or so, then wipe off all the excess. Remember, only the lube that gets into the chain's innards does any good; the rest just collects dirt. The fresh lube will help get rid of any extra grit that you'd didn't get the first time you wiped the chain clean.

Every so often, your chain may get so filthy that you have to remove it entirely and soak it in a jar of solvent to clean it. Use a chain-removal tool,

being careful not to drive the rivet all the way through. While the chain is off, clean the bike's chain rings, freewheel cogs, and derailleur pulleys, too. Another approach to cleaning your chain thoroughly (on the bike) is to use a Vetta or Allsop chain cleaner. Ask your bike shop about it.

Bicycle chains last about 1500–2000 miles (2500-3000 kilometers) before they wear out. They're cheap, so if yours gets rusty or really gritty, just replace it.

There are two more essential systems that you should know something about: brakes and derailleurs. If you're not sure how either or both of these systems work, put your bike on a work stand, turn the pedals, and operate the brakes or shift the gears, all the while watching how each separate part functions.

Most contemporary road bikes have sidepull brakes, which are pretty easy to adjust and maintain. To stop

your bike efficiently and safely, the brakes have to be adjusted properly. This means mainly two things: The cable has to be adjusted to the proper tension, and the brake shoes have to make proper contact with the rim.

First, be sure that when you apply the brakes, the lever doesn't come in all the way to the handlebars; otherwise, you might not be able to apply enough pressure on the rims to stop. As the new cables on your bike stretch and as the brake shoes wear, the levers will move closer to the handlebars. So every few months, you may need to loosen the bolt where the cable is attached to the brake caliper and pull the cable in tighter.

Steve Broaddus

Occasionally, your brake cables and pads will require a simple adjustment.

Steve Broaddus

Don't pull the cable too tight, though. If you don't allow enough play, the brakes will grab as soon as you pull the levers a little bit, minimizing your braking control. The other thing to watch is that your brake shoes (the parts that make contact with the rim) stay tight and aligned to the center of the rim. Periodically, check the tightness of the bolts that secure the shoes to the brake calipers. Brake cables and shoes last for years before they need replacing.

The final thing to keep tabs on are your bike's derailleurs, or gear changers. The purpose of both the front and rear derailleur is to move the chain from one chain ring to another, and from one freewheel cog to another, changing the gears to suit the terrain and your energy level. Modern derailleurs are very reliable and durable, and rarely go out of adjustment.

On both derailleurs, pay attention to the two *limit screws*. These limit their travel in both of the directions it can move, outward or in toward the bike's center. If the limit screws aren't set correctly on the rear derailleur, it will move the chain into the spokes, or lodge it between the small cog of the freewheel and the bike frame, or both; or, you won't be able to shift the chain over the full range of cogs. Look at the derailleur and freewheel from behind; when the chain is on the inner or outer cog, the derailleur arm and chain should form a vertical plane exactly in line with that cog. A misadjusted front derailleur will drop the chain off the inside of the small chain ring, off the outside of the large chain ring, or it won't shift properly from one chain ring to another.

Almost all quality bikes now have some sort of index shifting. These shifting systems, when properly adjusted, make it almost impossible to miss a shift; you simply pull back or push forward on the right (rear) shift lever until you hear and feel a "click," and the derailleur moves the chain into perfect alignment on the appropriate freewheel cog. Not only are these shifting systems easy to use, they're also fairly easy to keep in adjustment.

Indexed shifting systems all have barrel adjusters on the rear derailleur and shift levers with detents. Here's how to keep them shifting smoothly:

If you find that the rear derailleur isn't completing a shift when you move the lever, or if the shifts are noisy, put your bike on a repair stand. First, make sure the high- and low-gear adjustments on the rear derailleur are working properly by adjusting the limit screws (as indicated above). To do this, you need to put the shift lever in the "friction" mode.

Next, you can adjust the indexing. Shift the chain onto the smallest freewheel cog, and switch the shift lever back to the "index" mode. While turning the pedals, pull the rear derailleur back one detent to shift the chain on to the second freewheel cog. If the chain doesn't move to the second cog, turn the barrel adjuster counterclockwise (when looked at from the rear) to increase cable tension. If the chain shifts up to the third cog, turn the barrel adjuster clockwise to reduce tension on the cable.

When the chain shifts properly, again turn the barrel adjuster counterclockwise until the chain just begins to make contact with the third cog, then turn it clockwise to eliminate any clatter. Once you've completed this step, shift the chain through the whole gear range; each shift should be smooth and crisp.

Steve Broaddus

Derailleur adjustments are relatively simple. (Left) All indexed-shifting derailleurs have barrel adjusters at the rear to tighten or loosen cable tension. (Right) Screwdriver indicates high- and low-gear adjustment screws.

Steve Broaddus

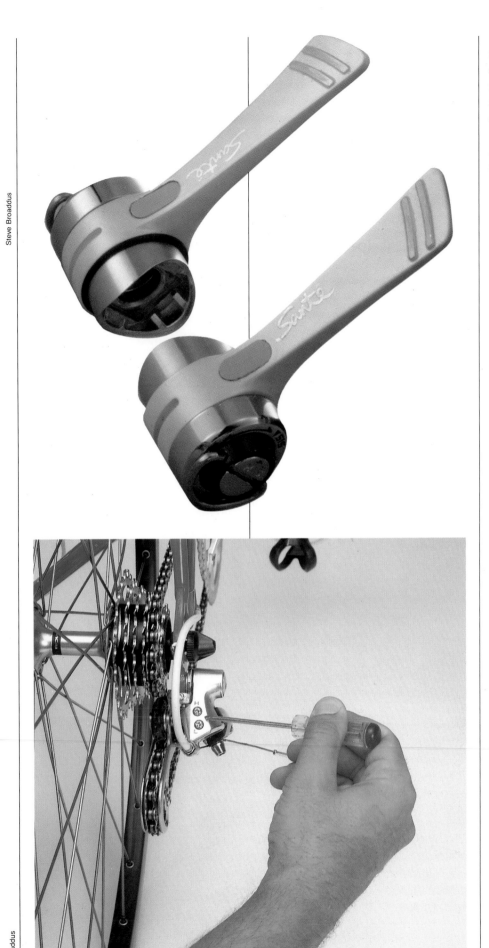

Steve Broaddus

In general, you won't need to adjust the cable tension very often—every couple thousand miles (or kilometers). Some manufacturers recommend that an indexed shifting derailleur's cable and housing be replaced once a season for best performance. If you find that your indexed shifting system goes out of adjustment frequently, take your bike to the shop to see whether the derailleur hanger is bent or the frame is out of alignment.

That's almost everything you need to know for basic bike maintenance. Every so often, check to see that all the nuts and bolts on your bike are tight. (The crank-fixing bolt on the crankset needs periodic tightening, for example.) Put an occasional drop of lubricant on all moving parts; if you ride in the rain frequently, you'll need to lube your bike more often (including a complete overhaul, because water will get into the internal bearings of the hubs, bottom bracket, and headset). Those bearings need periodic attention, too, as does the tension in the spokes of your wheels, but maintenance on these parts (assuming you don't abuse your bike) is far less frequent—once a year or so. It's also beyond the skills of casual mechanics and requires *lots* more tools.

If you buy a new bike, reputable shops will include a free thirty-day tune-up, at which time the shop's mechanics check over your bike after you've ridden it a while to make sure everything is properly adjusted. Your new bike may also have an owner's manual, which will explain some of these procedures in more detail. It's a good idea to give your bike a quick pre-ride inspection each time you go for a ride. Check the tires, brakes, derailleurs, and so on. Look the bike over quickly top to bottom, front to back. That way, you'll catch potential problems before they materialize.

A final tip: Use your ears as well as your eyes when caring for your bicycle. A bike that's adjusted correctly runs smoothly and silently. When you notice an unusual sound, it's a signal that something needs attending to. And if you're paid attention to everything that's been stated so far, you'll probably know how to fix it yourself.

GLOSSARY OF CYCLING TERMS

Aerobic—meaning literally "with oxygen," the exercise intensity level at which the body's oxygen needs are met. A conditioned athlete can continue aerobic exercise for long periods of time. (The opposite is anaerobic.)

Bottom bracket shell—a short, cylindrical lug in a bicycle frame to which the bottom bracket assembly (axle, fixed and adjustable cups, and ball bearings) and crankset are attached. It is located at the intersection of the down tube, the seat tube, and the chain stays.

Butted tubing—a type of tubing found in better-quality bike frames. The wall thickness of butted tubes is thin throughout the tubing, except at the ends, where it is thicker to provide strength at the points of intersection.

Cable—the wound or braided wire that regulates the movements of the derailleurs and brakes. Brake cable is surrounded by cable housing, as is the section of derailleur cable that runs from the chain stay to the rear derailleur.

Cadence—the rate of pedaling, measured by the number of revolutions completed by one foot.

Calipers—the parts of a brake activated by the brake levers, which press the brake shoes against the rims, stopping the bike. Calipers are the "arms" to which the brake shoes are attached.

Cantilever brake—the type of brake found on mountain and on some touring bikes. On cantilever brakes, the arms attach to the fork blades or chain stays, and are more rigid than the sidepull brakes typically found on road bikes.

Cardiovascular—relating to the heart, lungs and circulatory system.

Century—a 100-mile (160-kilometer) ride.

Chain stays—the two metal tubes on a bicycle's frame that are attached to the bottom bracket shell at one end and to the rear dropouts at the other.

Chainwheel—a part of the crankset. Chainwheels (or chainrings) are the toothed wheels that, along with the freewheel, provide the means for a bicycle's forward motion and determine its gearing.

Chrome-molybdenum—a high-strength steel alloy used in the construction of quality bicycle frames.

Cleat—an adjustable metal or plastic fitting on the sole of a bike shoe that either engages a conventional pedal cage (used with toe clips and straps) or is inserted into a clipless/strapless pedal system.

Clincher (wired-on) tire—a type of tire with a separate inner tube, used on the vast majority of production bicycles.

Components—the parts of a bicycle that are attached to the frame.

Crankset—a component made up of several parts that is fitted to a bicycle's bottom bracket shell, usually consisting of two or three chainwheels and two crankarms. The pedals might also be considered a part of the crankarm assembly.

Criterium bicycle—a type of racing bicycle used in a race covering numerous laps of a course about one mile long. It is very rigid and responsive.

Derailleur (front and rear)—the gear-shifting components that move the chain from one chainwheel or freewheel cog to another, as a result of the rider pulling or pushing a shift lever.

Down tube—the tube in a bicycle frame that runs from the head tube to the bottom bracket shell.

Drafting—taking advantage of the windbreak created by another rider by riding close to his back wheel.

Drive train——the components directly involved with making a bicycle's rear wheel turn (the crankset, chain, pedals, derailleurs and freewheel).

Dropouts—metal connection points (lugs) to the front and rear wheels. Front dropouts are attached to the ends of the fork blades; rear dropouts are attached to the chain and seat stays.

Fork—the part of the bicycle frame consisting of two fork blades, which are attached to the front drop-outs, a fork crown, and a steerer tube, which fits inside the head tube, and to which the headset is attached.

Fork rake—the perpendicular measurement from the center line of the fork to the center of the dropout, usually between 1 and 2½ inches. The fork rake, in conjunction with head tube angle, affects steering responsiveness and stability.

Frame—the principal structural element of a bicycle, consisting of three main tubes (top, seat, and down), a head tube, a fork, seat stays, chain stays, and dropouts.

Frame geometry—a property of the bicycle frame determined by its specific dimensions, including the tubing lengths and the angles at which the tubing is joined. Frame geometry determines a bike's handling qualities to a great degree.

Freewheel—the set of five, six or seven toothed rings (cogs) threaded or splined onto the rear hub of a derailleur bicycle. The number of teeth on the cogs, in conjunction with those on the chainwheels, determine a bicycle's gearing.

Head tube—the short, vertical tube on the front of a bicycle frame into which the fork and handlebar stem are fitted. The top tube and down tube are attached to the head tube.

Head tube angle—the complement of angle formed by the intersection of the head tube and top tube, usually measuring between 68 and 75 degrees. The head tube angle is important in determining a bike's steering characteristics.

Headset—a component consisting of two sets of bearing racks and ball bearings, attached to the fork, and at either end and inside of the head tube. Responsible for the smooth turning of the steering mechanism.

Hub—the front or rear wheel bearing unit which has been drilled to receive spokes. Those spokes are attached (laced) to the rim. A hub contains an axle and bearings.

Indexed shifting—a new, more precise method of shifting gears, in which pulling back or pushing forward on the shift lever for the rear derailleur is accompanied by an audible "click" that you can also feel. This results in the precise movement of the chain to the next larger or smaller freewheel cog.

Intervals—a training method of alternating hard, short periods of riding with easier periods of recovery.

Long, steady distance (LSD)—a training term meaning rides usually of two or more hours at a steady aerobic rate, generally at approximately 75 percent of maximum heart rate.

Lug—a part of a bicycle's frame. Stamped steel, cast steel or aluminum pieces into which the frame tubes are fitted, joining the bike frame into a single unit.

Manganese-molybdenum—a high-strength steel alloy used in the construction of quality bicycle frames.

Overtraining—a condition of excessive mental and/or physical fatigue, caused by an extended period of hard riding to which the body has not had time to adapt.

Quadriceps—the set of large muscles on the front of the upper thigh.

Quick-release—levers on a bicycle's hubs that secure the wheel to the dropouts; quick-release hubs can be tightened or loosened with the flick of a lever. Mountain bikes also have quick-release seat post levers.

Rim—a circular band of aluminum alloy, attached by spokes to a hub and on which is mounted a tire and tube.

Seat cluster—a three-way lug, into which the seat and top tubes are fitted, and to which the seat stays are attached by means of a finely adjustable clamping.

Seat post—a hollow cylinder that fits into the seat cluster, to which the saddle is attached by means of a finely adjustable clamping mechanism.

Seat stays—the two metal tubes of a bike's frame that are connected to the seat cluster at one end and to the rear dropout at the other.

Seat tube—the tube in a bicycle frame running from the seat cluster lug to the bottom bracket shell. A bicycle's size is measured in inches or centimeters along the seat tube from the center of the bottom bracket to the center or top of the top tube.

Seat tube angle—the acute angle at the point that the seat tube intersects the top tube. Seat tube angle, to a degree, determines the fore-aft position of the rider in relation to the pedal spindle (axle), and affects the rider's pedaling motion and weight distribution.

Stem—the aluminum alloy part that holds the handlebars, the bottom of which is inserted into the steerer tube.

Time trial—a race against the clock in which riders usually start at one-minute intervals. Group riding tactics, such as drafting, are not allowed.

Toe clips—the steel, aluminum alloy or plastic encasements that fit over a rider's forefoot. Used with toe straps, they secure a rider's feet to the pedals.

Top tube—the tube in a bicycle frame that attaches to the head tube and the seat cluster lug, roughly parallel to the ground. Its length affects a rider's torso and arm position.

Training effect—positive physiological adaptation to exercise by the body, including increased lung capacity, stronger heart, reduced resting pulse, increased size and number of blood vessels, improved muscle tone, reduced body fat, increased energy, and increased ability to process oxygen.

True—a property of wheels, referring to their concentric (roundness) and lateral (side-to-side) alignment.

Tubular (sew-up) tire—a lightweight tire usually used for racing, which has its inner tube permanently sewn inside the casing. It requires a special type of rim, to which it is glued.

Wheelbase—the distance between the front and rear dropouts; the length of the wheelbase affects a bike's handling properties, especially its turning ability.

APPENDICES

BOOKS

Many books have been written about bicycles and bicycling. Here are some of the better ones:

Anybody's Bike Book, by Tom Cuthbertson, Ten Speed Press, Berkeley, California, 1984. A classic. Good, basic information about fixing your bike (and much more), written in a humorous and sympathetic tone by a Right-Thinking Cyclist. Hilarious drawings.

Back Country Bikepacking, by William Sanders, Stackpole Books, Harrisburg, Pennsylvania, 1982. Complete guide to bikepacking, by a thoroughly experienced bicycle tourist.

The Complete Cycle Sport Guide, by Peter Konopka, EP Publishing Ltd., England, 1982. Brief yet informative book on riding technique and training to race.

Effective Cycling, by John Forester, MIT Press, Cambridge, Massachusetts, 1984. Without a doubt the most authoritative manual on how to ride safely and sanely. Filled with good general information; if you only buy one other book on bicycling, this should be it.

Living on Two Wheels, by Dennis Coello, Ross Books, Berkeley, California, 1983. Covers buying a bike, bike safety, bike mechanics, commuting, and touring advice. Probably most valuable for the latter two.

Richard's Bicycle Book, Richard Ballantine, Ballantine Books, New York City, 1982. Good general information, but primarily a maintenance book. Good diagrams.

CYCLING MAGAZINES

Bicycling, Rodale Press, 33 E. Minor Street, Emmaus, Pennsylvania 18049. The oldest, largest, and best general interest magazine on the sport.

Bicycle Guide, 711 Boylston Street, Boston, Massachusetts 02116. General interest cycling magazine with an emphasis on products and bike testing.

Bicycle U.S.A., The bulletin of the League of American Wheelmen (L.A.W.); good source of information on bicycle clubs, recreational riding and cycling politics.

Cyclist, 20916 Higgins Court, Torrance, California 90501. General interest cycling magazine.

The Fat-Tire Flyer, P.O. Box 757, Fairfax, California 94930. Insider's guide to mountain biking.

Mountain Bike, P.O. Box 989, Crested Butte, Colorado 81224.

Mountain Bike Action, 10600 Sepulveda Boulevard, Mission Hills, California 91345.

Winning—Bicycle Racing Illustrated, 1127 Hamilton Street, Allentown, Pennsylvania 18102. A magazine devoted to bicycle racing.

CYCLING ORGANIZATIONS

American Youth Hostels, Inc. (AYH), 1332 "I" Street, N.W., Washington, D.C. 20005. Supports local and European bicycle touring.

Bicycle Federation, 1055 Thomas Jefferson Street, N.W., Washington, D.C. 20007. Bicycle activist group.

League of American Wheelmen, 10 E. Read Street, P.O. 988, Baltimore, Maryland 21203. A national cycling organization serving the interests of touring, commuting and recreational cyclists.

Bikecentennial, P.O. Box 8308, Missoula, Montana 59807. A national service organization for touring cyclists, which provides maps, routing, and touring information. Publishers of *Bicycle Forum* and *Bikecentennial News*.

National Off-Road Bicycle Association, P.O. Box 1901, Chandler, Arizona 85244. This organization covers all aspects of mountain biking.

United States Cycling Federation, 1750 E. Boulder, Colorado Springs, Colorado 80909. The governing body of amateur competitive cycling in the United States.

IMPORTANT BICYCLE PARTS

1. Drop handlebars
2. Side pull brakes
3. Light-but-strong alloy rims
4. Quill or platform pedals
5. Rear derailleur
6. Front derailleur
7. Double or triple crankset
8. Shift levers
9. Brake levers
10. Freewheel
11. Clincher or tubular tires
12. Quick-release axles
13. Seat post
14. Stem
15. Chain

Don Lauritzen/Courtesy of Nishiki Bicycle Co.

MAJOR BICYCLE MANUFACTURERS

Benotto
2260 Main St., Suite 8
Chula Vista, CA 92001

Bianchi
385 Oyster Pt. Blvd. #6
South San Francisco, CA 94080

Bridgestone
15003 Wicks Blvd.
San Leandro, CA 94557

Cannondale
9 Brookside Place
Georgetown, CT 06829

Centurion, Diamond Back
WSI
1837 De Havilland Drive
Newbury Park, CA 91320

Cinelli
Primo International
10335 Landsbury, Suite 316
Houston, TX 77099

CIÖCC
Veltec-Boyer
1793 Catalina
Sand City, CA 93955

Colnago
Celo Europa
1575 W. Broadway
Anaheim, CA 92802

Cunningham
Wilderness Trail
121 Wood Lane
Fairfax, CA 94930

Cycles Gitane USA
3 Union Drive
Olney, IL 62450

Davidson
Bill Davidson Cycles
2116 Western Ave.
Seattle, WA 98121

De Rosa, Eddy Merckx, Pinarello
Gita Sporting Goods
8107 Arrowridge #M
Charlotte, NC 28210

Fat City Cycles
331 Somerville Ave.
Somerville, MA 02143

Fisher Mountain Bikes
1421 Francisco Blvd.
San Rafael, CA 94901

Fuji
Toshoku America
P.O. Box 60
118 Bauer Drive
Oakland, NJ 07436

Bruce Gordon
1070 W. Second St.
Eugene, OR 97402

Guerciotti, Rossin, Tommaso
Ten Speed Drive
131 Tomahawk Drive, Unit 6
Indian Harbour Beach, FL 32937

Ibis
P.O. Box 275
Sebastopol, CA 95472

Jamis
Cycles USA
3000 Commonwealth Ave
Tallahassee, FL 32303

KHS
1264 E. Walnut
Carson, CA 90746

Klein
207 S. Prairie
Chehalis, WA 98532

Lotus
P.O. Box 3
Syosset, NY 11791

Mangusta, Mongoose
BMX Products
1250 Avenida DiCaso, Suite H
Camarillo, CA 93010

Masi
Cicli Masi
P.O. Box 1653
San Marcos, CA 92069

Miele
1869 Sismet Road
Mississauga, Ontario, Canada

Montaneus
P.O. Box 1245
St. Cloud, MN 56302

Dave Moulton
P.O. Box 1075
San Marcos, CA 92069

Nishiki
West Coast Cycle
717 Artesia Blvd.
Carson, CA 90746

Olmo
Bicycle Parts Pacific
P.O. Box 640
Santee, CA 92071

Panasonic
1 Panasonic Way
Secaucus, NJ 07094

Peugeot
555 Gotham Parkway
Carlstadt, NJ 07072

Raleigh
22710 72nd St. South
Kent, WA 98032

3Rensho
Ariel Trading Co.
24 North Few St.
Madison, WI 53703

Ritchey USA
1326 Hancock St.
Redwood City, CA 94061

Ross
P.O. Box 147
Rockaway Beach, NY 11693

Richard Sachs
Main St.
Chester, CT 06412

Salsa Cycles
110 Howard St.
Petaluma, CA 94952

Santana Tandems
P.O. Box 1205
Claremont, CA 91711

Schwinn
217 Jefferson St.
Chicago, IL 60606

Serotta
Grange Road
Greenfield Center, NY 12833

Shogun
Seattle Bike Supply
1109 Andover Park West
Seattle, WA 98188

Specialized
15130 Concord Circle
Morgan Hill, CA 95037

Terry
140 Despatch Dr.
East Rochester, NY 14445

Trek
801 W. Madison St.
Waterloo, WI 52594

Univega
Lawee, Inc.
3030 Walnut Ave.
Long Beach, CA 90807

MAJOR COMPONENT MANUFACTURERS

Campagnolo USA
43 Fairfield Place
West Caldwell, NJ 07006

Shimano American Corp.
1 Shimano Drive
Irvine, CA 92718

SunTour
2 Cranberry Road
Parsippany, NJ 07054

BICYCLE TOOLS

Park Tool Co.
2250 White Bear Ave.
St. Paul, MN 55109

United Bicycle Tool Supply
12225 Highway 66
Ashland, OR 97520

BICYCLE CLOTHING MANUFACTURERS

Alitta
75 Spring St.
New York, NY 10022

Avenir
WSI
1837 DeHavilland Drive
Newbury Park, CA 91320

Avocet
P.O. Box 7615
Menlo Park, CA 94025

Bellwether
1161 Mission St.
San Francisco, CA 94103

BlackBottoms
P.O. Box 7104
Salt Lake City, UT 84107

Brancale, Tommaso
Ten Speed Drive Imports
131 Tomahawk Drive, Unit 6
Indian Harbour Beach, FL 32937

Cannondale
9 Brookside Place
Georgetown, CT 06829

Descente America
601 Madison Ave.
New York, NY 10022

Emily K Sportswear
539 State St.
Santa Barbara, CA 93101

J.T. Actif
P.O. Box 762
Millburn, NJ 07041

Lake Sport
1015 Davis
Evanston, IL 60201

Nike
9000 S.W. Nimbus
Beaverton, OR 97005

Pearl Izumi USA
3630 Pearl St.
Boulder, CO 80301

Rhode Gear
765 Allens Ave.
Providence, RI 01905

Vigorelli
2200 Adeline St., Suite 250
Oakland, CA 94607